First published in English in 2007
by Merrell Publishers Limited

Head office
81 Southwark Street
London SE1 0HX

New York office
49 West 24th Street, 8th Floor
New York, NY 10010

merrellpublishers.com

First published as *Frauen, die schreiben, leben gefährlich*
in 2006 by Elisabeth Sandmann Verlag GmbH, Munich
Copyright © 2006 Elisabeth Sandmann Verlag GmbH
Illustrations copyright © 2006 the copyright holders;
see p. 152

English-language edition copyright © 2007 Merrell
    Publishers Limited
Foreword copyright © 2007 Francine Prose

British Library Cataloguing-in-Publication Data:
Bollmann, Stefan
Women who write
1. Women authors 2. Literature – Women authors –
History and criticism
I. Title
809.8'9287

ISBN-13: 978-1-8589-4375-6
ISBN-10: 1-8589-4375-2

Translated by Helen Atkins
Edited by Kirsty Seymour-Ure

Printed and bound in Italy

Jacket, front: Virginia Woolf (see p. 89)
Jacket, back (left to right): Dorothy Parker (see p. 118);
    Toni Morrison (see p. 140); Colette (see p. 82)
Endpapers: Colette writing, undated photograph
p. 4: Letter from Elizabeth I to duc d'Anjou, 1579
p. 5: Manuscript of "Gondal Poems" by Emily Brontë,
    February 1844
pp. 150–51: Colette, photograph, 1909

Stefan Bollmann

Women Who Write

Foreword by Francine Prose

MERRELL
LONDON · NEW YORK

Mô trescher, si la chose longuement attendue fust esté bonne, quant elle arriva, ie eusse esté mieulx satisfaicte de la longue attente qu'il a pleu a Stafford me prester. Mais voyant que la paix bible qu'a peine faicte, ie me voy trop de rayson qui fuste ba demeurée. Sinon qu'il m'a faict a croire qu'il ba faict par vostre commandement a quoy i'ay saincte volunté qu'il obaye. Et ayant tout a ceste heure receu lettres de france que le Roy prolonge ceste paix soubs quelque difficultés qui me pourrot trop tost coustsuire. Ie serois tresayse qu'on laissast s'esbahir de so longue arrest, me asseurant que quelque temps s'en fust leur venue. Et pour la cause du Roy de Navarre & ba partie ce ioy ie prendray la sardi 66. Ie vous dire qu'il vous touchera bien prens en reputation que ne le laissast en pire estat qu'ilz furent au commencement de ces nouveaulx troubles. Car si leur plus grandes bourtés leur fussent arrachés comme si feroient y du Roy adioustant que le Roy mesme me manda dire par so ambassadeur qu'il ne feur miroit la premiere pacificatio et ne demanderoit sino les villes & lieux, n'ou villernit pris. Et pour ie pardonners la curiosité qui me tient en vos actions & qui ie souhait tout l'heur & toreur qui peut arriver a la perpetuell...

Emily Jane Brontë.   Transcribed February 2nd 1844

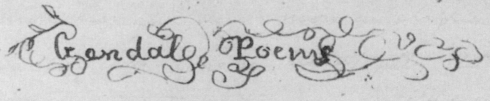

Gondal Poems

A. G. A.   March 6th 1837

There shines the moon, at noon of night.
Vision of Glory - Dream of light!
Holy as heaven - undimmed and pure,
Looking down on the lonely moor -
And lonelier still beneath her ray
That drear moor stretches far away

Till it seems strange that aught can lie
Beyond its zone of silver sky =

Bright moon - dear moon! when years have past
My weary feet return at last -
And still upon Lake Elnor's breast
Thy solemn rays serenely rest
And still on Elnor's sighing wave
Like murmurs over Elbü's grave
And Earth's the same but Oh to see
How wildly Time has altered me!
Am I the being who long ago
Sat watching by that water side
The light of life expiring slow
From his fair cheek and brow of pride?
Not oft these mountains feel the shine
Of such a day - as fading then,
Cast from its front of gold divine
A last smile on the heathery plain
And kissed the far off peaks of snow
That gleaming on the horizon shine

CONTENTS

Francine Prose

FOREWORD

A writer, any writer, is dangerous enough. The guests are always overjoyed when the musicians show up at the party, but when the writer walks into the room, the voices grow ever so slightly hushed. Perhaps the partygoers fear they might be overheard, and that their careless conversation might some day flow from the mouth of a character in a novel. They begin to behave themselves, foreseeing and dreading that moment when they open a book and find their bad conduct appearing, only thinly disguised, as the turning point in some unfortunate fictional hero's downfall.

But when that writer is a woman, when it's a woman who has crashed the party, how much greater the fear and dread. How much more shaming the possibility that one's misbehavior—or even the simple, straightforward facts of one's life—might be noticed, recorded, documented, and even judged by a female—a lesser being! For everything that a woman is traditionally supposed to be—retiring, submissive, reassuringly unobservant, endlessly forgiving, deaf, dumb, and blind, and in every way (especially with regard to matters of the intellect) inferior to the most ordinary, average male—is precisely the opposite of the personal qualities required to be a writer, of the penetrating intelligence and the hyperalert sensibility of the artist in general, and of the author in particular.

The essential subversiveness of women's writing may be part of the reason why, throughout history, so many works by women have been undervalued and under-recognized. What better way to disarm something that threatens you, that challenges the larger culture, than to claim that it is inferior, narrow, trivial, shallow, overly domestic, frivolous, and in every important way less serious than a corresponding work by a man? We dismiss as sentimental Harriet Beecher Stowe's *Uncle Tom's Cabin*, conveniently forgetting its not insignificant role in helping to start the American Civil War. Even as little boys, male readers frequently learn that such books as those in Astrid Lindgren's Pippi

Longstocking series—with their headlong, joyous attack on authority, pomposity, and the strictures placed upon little girls—were intended primarily for their sisters and female cousins.

In her beautiful essay on the life and work of Charlotte Brontë, one of the most sympathetic pieces ever written by one writer, or one woman, or one human being, about another, Rebecca West reflects on those aspects of the earlier novelist's subject matter that have made it problematic (and simultaneously thrilling) for generations of readers:

> She records oppressions practiced by the dowered upon the dowerless, and by adults on children, and seems to many of her readers absurd and unpleasant when she does so; but that is perhaps not because such incidents never happen, but because we dislike admitting that they happen. There is hardly a more curious example of the gap we leave between life and literature than the surprise and incredulity recorded by successive generations of Brontëan commentators at the passages in the sisters' works which suggest that the well-to-do are sometimes uncivil to their employees.
>
> *Rebecca West: A Celebration*, 1977

Reading this, we cannot help but feel that we understand why—apart from the garden-variety manners and mores of the "man's country" that West calls Victorian England—Charlotte Brontë and her sisters might have chosen to adopt, and publish under, male pseudonyms.

If there is anything that the wide range of women collected in this volume have in common—besides their literary talent, and secondly their gender—it's a certain bravery, or an unkillable impulse, or whatever it was that impelled them to put that first word down on paper, and then the next and the next.

It's never easy to write, but it must have been harder for them. Few women are born to parents who naturally assume and boast, with confidence and pride, that their newborn baby daughter *will grow up to be a writer*! Few women receive the easy and welcoming encouragement of their male colleagues, more of whom are likely to agree with the poet Heinrich Heine, quoted in this book as saying that women's writing is marred by "a certain kind of malicious gossip, a cliquishness that they import into literature." Few women *can* put down a single word without first clawing through (or finding a crafty way around) the thicket created by other people's expectations about what they should be and do, about the primacy of their "biological" role as nurturers and caretakers, wives and mothers and daughters. Why would anyone want to write a book when she can have a baby?

Each of the lives—and bodies of work—highlighted in this volume represents a triumph over the forces that every writer, and women writers in particular, must overcome in the effort to write so much as one sentence, let alone a sustained and cohesive narrative.

Consider the courage and imagination it must have taken to be Mary Wollstonecraft, to pull oneself up from a childhood marked by what we have learned to call extreme "downward mobility," to struggle to help care for an unfortunate mother and siblings, to be an autodidact, to work as a governess, to find a mentor and model, and to invent (or ally oneself with) a whole new way of life, to entertain and realize the radical idea of being an independent woman and a female intellectual. And in the midst of all that, to write fiction and essays and polemics, a book of *Thoughts on the Education of Daughters* and, most famously, *A Vindication of the Rights of Woman*.

Consider the very different sort of bravery it must have taken to be Jane Austen, to see more than you are meant to see, to turn a profoundly sympathetic but nonetheless unfemininely cool eye on the ambitions and failed hopes, the hearts and minds, of one's neighbors. Or, for that matter, consider the nearly unimaginable stamina, optimism, and resolve that it took to survive, as Anne Frank did, with no privacy, no space, not one moment of freedom from intense and justified anxiety about one's very life—in other words, to operate under the most impossible conditions for the birth and growth of a writer—and nevertheless to become one, at a prodigiously early age, and to produce a work of genius. We can only marvel at the nerve it requires even now to be Arundhati Roy, seizing every available opportunity to speak out against the powerful and terrifyingly efficient forces that threaten our human rights and the future of our planet, daring to provoke the rage of one's own government and of its political and economic allies. Such stories remind us of how often, in women's lives, necessity and conscience are among the most influential of the muses.

Looking at the Cubist portrait of Anna Akhmatova (opposite), you may find yourself thinking of the famous story about how, in 1939, the poet stood in line outside the central prison in Leningrad, along with a crowd of other women, all of them carrying packages of food that they were trying to get to imprisoned relatives. Her only son, Lev Gumilyov, had been sent to a labor camp. A woman who recognized Akhmatova asked, "Can you describe this?" and the poet answered, "Yes, I can." The result was her remarkable poem "Requiem," which, you might say, proved as dangerous to the totalitarian regime as other, more obviously political plots or protests against its cruelty and power.

The list of writers whose names appear here includes the famous (Simone de Beauvoir, Toni Morrison, Virginia Woolf, Germaine de Staël) and those who are less well known (Lilli Jahn, Božena Němcová, Madeleine de Scudéry) but nonetheless worthy of being remembered and honored. And there are a few who, like Irène Némirovsky, had literary reputations during their lives that have continued to grow long after they were silenced.

ANNA AKHMATOVA (1889–1966)
Painting by N.I. Altman (1889–1970), 1914

The gallery of women includes not only artistic but also political heroines, even martyrs: for example, Sophie Scholl, who wrote and distributed leaflets as part of her work with the White Rose, a nonviolent movement dedicated to resisting the Nazis. She was caught and executed in 1943.

Studying these women's portraits, one after another, inspires pride and respect, as well as tenderness and sympathy for the sacrifices and hardships that, for them, so clearly and inevitably accompanied the often less tangible rewards of creation. How beautiful these faces are—young and old, black and white, from every continent—and how intriguing, intelligent, and, above all, *individual* are the gazes that meet ours as we turn the pages!

The example of Sylvia Plath is both cautionary and inspiring, with its parable-like narrative about the fierce insistence on making something of great beauty despite, or perhaps even because of, one's demons, struggling fiercely against them until—in Plath's case—the demons win out. And one keeps returning to the photos of Colette and of Karen Blixen, two women who simply refused to take the safe, traditional route. Both were extraordinary not only for their literary abilities, but also for resisting every pressure to limit themselves or more narrowly circumscribe their participation in life, to enact the conventional roles that women were (and still are) encouraged to assume.

One of the most interesting things about the present volume is the window it opens on to the lives of the writers of books for children, women we might imagine living in a world as sheltered and sunny as the climates they describe in their books. But that was hardly true of the career of Johanna Spyri, the Swiss-born author of the beloved children's classic *Heidi* (or, as we learn here, *Heidi's Years of Learning and Travel*). Spyri struggled with severe depression, and later had to cope with the early death of her only son. And while the life of Beatrix Potter was apparently tranquil enough, it was also exceedingly lonely. Potter spent much of her early life in her family's home with her parents, who obliged her to run their household and disapproved of her engagement to a young man, who in any case died before they could marry. Nonetheless, she managed to write more than twenty books, to marry finally at the age of forty-seven, and to amass so much farmland (presumably inhabited by the creatures that populated her books) that, on her death in 1943, she left four thousand acres to the preservation society the National Trust.

Some years ago, I had the experience of writing a magazine piece in which I suggested that the playing field was still far from level for most (if not all) contemporary women writers. I looked at the different ways in which a literary work is approached and read solely because of the name (male or female) that appears on the title page, and at the disparity between the respect—as evidenced by literary prizes and prestigiously placed book reviews—commonly given to male authors and that accorded to women writers. I found a dispiriting number of near-contemporary male writers and critics all too willing to echo (and outdo) the dismissive view of Heinrich Heine, quoted above.

In writing the essay, I had imagined that I was helpfully pointing out what everyone else must have noticed but, for some reason, never bothered to say. I assumed that I would be thanked by grateful women authors and by male readers vowing to mend their ways and read literature by women with a more open mind. In fact, nothing could have been further from the way things turned out. The essay aroused a furious controversy, fueled, on the one hand, by men denying that the gender gap existed, and on the other by women angered by the suggestion (which I had never made) that a quota system be enforced for the distribution of awards and attention. Still, ever so briefly, the situation for women improved, and I like to think that I was partly responsible for the fact that one saw more women's names in the tables of contents

BEATRIX POTTER (1866–1943)
Photograph, 1907

of major American magazines. And then things seemed to slip backward again, to some default position where everything goes on, the same as it has always gone for women—that is to say, their task is simply *harder*—and everyone politely agrees not to notice.

Which is why a book such as this one seems valuable and worth having. The mention of these writers and the accounts of their careers remind us of how many women, in every age, transcended (or ignored) the traditional barriers that have tried to keep their work from being written, published, and read. This book reminds us that the ability to describe the world or to create another world, to tell the truth or to invent a higher truth worth telling, has, after all, everything to do with talent and intelligence, spirit and soul, and nothing to do with our reproductive organs. We will continue to need books such as this until that fact seems as obvious, as self-evident, as it is.

Introduction

THE FIGHT WITH THE ANGEL

D o women have a different way of writing? Certainly they once wrote under very different conditions from men. The view expressed by the Austrian author Marie von Ebner-Eschenbach (1830–1916) that "when a woman learned to read ... the issue of women's rights was born" is even more true of writing than of reading. For far longer than men, the majority of women were semiliterate: They could read but not write. It took them even longer to win the freedom to choose what they wanted to read. And they had to fight longest of all to gain the sort of acknowledgment for their writing that generally was, and still is, accorded to men as a matter of course, especially if they wanted their writing to be more than an occasional pastime. Is the question of women's status settled and done with? Or is it still there, but in a different form?

Simone de Beauvoir described women as "the second sex." Her celebrated study of women's status and self-image in history and the present day appeared in 1949. In it, she exhorted women writers not to be content with being amateurs; spontaneity alone was not enough. If women did not have the courage and stamina to make something of themselves in the world, their sensibility would never be more than sterile vanity. Of the legions of women "who flirt with literature or art, only a few stick at it," de Beauvoir wrote. "And even the ones who get over that first hurdle often remain torn between narcissism and an inferiority complex." Nowadays, almost two generations later, more and more professional women writers find it insulting to be treated differently—even if that means preferentially—on the grounds of their sex. Most would like to be able to identify with what the French writer Marguerite Yourcenar said of her own career: that at a certain point she ceased to be a woman who wrote and became primarily an author—an author who was also a

People say I'm an egoist.
I'm a fighter.

Ethel Smyth

woman. But whereas in the case of most male authors their sex is of little relevance to the way they are perceived, women writers still have to be prepared to see their work judged in the light of their femaleness. I know a good many women who feel they are subject to a kind of positive discrimination, and would much rather set aside their predilections and characteristics as women than constantly have to put up with special treatment. Yet much, if not everything, depends on the social, political, and cultural context. It makes a big difference whether I raise the issue of women's rights as a member of a society dominated by, for example, an authoritarian form of Islam, or whether I do so as a citizen of a Western country where critical thinking and the freedom of the individual are more or less taken for granted. The risks facing a woman who opts to become an independent professional author in present-day Europe or North America relate to the practical problem of earning a living and also to what might be described as the existential insecurity of the writer. By contrast, a woman writer in Iran may face an immediate threat to her life, body, and soul in a repressive society that is very far from according equal rights to women.

Except in the final chapter, which introduces seven contemporary representatives of world literature, I have mostly drawn my gallery of writers from the last two hundred and fifty years of European and American culture. A juxtaposition of different periods can be beneficial: If we take a historical view of our own culture, we may gain greater insight into the processes and struggles taking place at the present time in other parts of the world and possibly closer to home, too. Thinking about other periods might even have relevance for our own behavior and the way we think about ourselves, for we may still be harboring attitudes that really belong to a previous age.

42/50   Edgar Holloway

VIRGINIA WOOLF (1882–1941)
Undated lithograph by Edgar Holloway (b. 1914)
Private collection

The feminine culture of the novel

Toward the end of the eighteenth century, when, in the spirit of the Enlightenment, the German writer on human relations Baron von Knigge offered the good citizens of his day a code of practical advice for living, he thought it proper to forbid "ladies" to take up writing as a profession and, as he put it, roam at will in the realms of learning. In educated middle-class circles, women could read and write. But this raised the question of what degree of professionalism in the world of letters should be permitted to the second sex. And here Knigge offered women little encouragement. How dare they, he protested, suddenly expect to have a voice and pass judgment on matters that since time immemorial had been the exclusive preserve of men? Women's ambitions in this regard could be the result only of female vanity, since most of them surely lacked the necessary ability. Of the forty or fifty women authors then writing in Germany, barely a dozen, in the baron's judgment, had what it took to be professional writers.

And yet, a well-disposed modern reader might object, a dozen is not bad. Was (or indeed is) the ratio of mediocrity to excellence so very much better among male authors? Not at all, Knigge readily admits. But one cannot make such a straightforward comparison, he adds, laying the foundation for a line of argument that is still used to defend male bastions even today. The undeniable fact that among male writers, too, only a few stand out from the crowd can be easily explained and excused: The rest are probably drawn to the profession by such common human weaknesses as a desire for fame or money. The same excuse will not do, however, for the less gifted among women writers. Women have to be better at the same métier because they are in the position of having to prove to men that they can do it at all.

Knigge was reacting to a new trend associated with reading and writing that emerged during the eighteenth century, one that was linked to changes in the economic field. Women now had more time and leisure. Increasingly, the necessities of everyday living were manufactured and could be bought at the market or in shops. In more affluent urban circles, at least, women's lives were no longer dominated by such domestic duties as sewing, spinning, weaving, baking bread, cooking, and making candles and soap. As early as 1713, an essay in a short-lived London periodical, *The Guardian*, argued that *belles-lettres*—such things as essays, criticism, and literature—belonged more to the world of women than to that of men. The first reason given for this was that women "have more spare Time upon their Hands, and lead a more Sedentary Life."

From the outset, the genre of the novel was linked to the emergence of a culture of reading among women. Even today the great majority of novel-readers are women. If they decided to imitate men and spend their leisure time surfing the internet, for example, there would soon be no money to be made from writing or publishing novels. The extraordinary rise of the novel in modern times is due, according to the author Henry James, to the extraordinary rise of women.

James's assertion is less true of the *writing* of novels. In the eighteenth century, most novels were indeed written by women, but women were not the leaders in terms of quality. That state of affairs was to change with Jane Austen, who created a synthesis of the two main strands in the evolving genre of the novel.

The model for one of these strands had been established by Samuel Richardson with his epistolary novels, including *Clarissa, or The History of a Young Lady* (1747–49). This type of novel, in the form of an exchange of letters, allowed the reader to enter deeply into the mind of the heroine, to the point of identifying completely, in Clarissa's case, with her difficult situation and her vacillation between resistance and compliance. In the eighteenth century, letter-writing was the main form by which women could express themselves on paper. In this area, they were often superior to their male correspondents, particularly when it came to describing emotions, and so it was chiefly women who established the conventions of this particular form of social culture. For many of them, moreover, the writing and exchanging of letters became a bridge leading to the writing of literature. The epistolary novel was thus by no means conjured out of thin air. On the contrary, the ground was already well prepared. Richardson made the epistolary novel an instrument for the study and portrayal of hitherto unrecognized aspects and unexplored depths of the human psyche. His model provided inspiration for many other works, including, in Germany, for example, Goethe's *The Sorrows of Young Werther*, published in 1774.

The other strand in the development of the novel is best represented by the works of Henry Fielding—especially *The History of Tom Jones, a Foundling* (1749)—in which psychological empathy is less important than the humorous depiction of external social reality. The authors of epistolary novels always kept themselves in the background, in the interests of the authenticity of their portrayal, as though they were following the movements of their protagonists with hidden microphones and telephoto lenses. Fielding, on the other hand, constantly intervenes in the events he describes. His aim is to present the reader with a rational interpretation of the narrative of life, with all its more-or-less improbable developments. He is less intent on eavesdropping on the human soul than on describing and explaining social behavior. The fact that the protagonists of epistolary novels were mostly women, while those of social novels were mostly men, exactly mirrors the different roles of the sexes at that time: What women lacked in worldly and practical experience, they made up for in the cultivation of a rich emotional life.

Jane Austen—we come to her at last—achieved, for the first time, a harmonious fusion of these two types of novel. In her works, the portrayal of the characters' inner consciousness and the author's critical observation of life merge seamlessly to produce a subtle interplay of empathy and distance, so that the complexities of human relationships are shown in both their psychological and their social aspects. It is significant that the first version of what is probably Austen's most celebrated novel, *Pride and Prejudice* (1813), was written in epistolary form. Later she realized that this literary device stood in the way of her wish to be present as the author in her novels—commenting on events, if not directly then certainly indirectly—and found that she was

perfectly able to portray realistic characters, with all their contradictions, without using the epistolary form. She achieves this through the dialogue in which her figures constantly engage; it is by what they say and their manner of saying it that their feelings and personalities, as well as their social roles, are revealed to us.

Austen lets us see how the individual's inner life and outward behavior—emotions, utterances, actions—relate to each other, complement or contradict each other, and reveal honesty or dishonesty, decisiveness, or thoughtlessness. Her characters are defined by their reaction to the situation in which they find themselves, rather than by a past with which the reader has first to be familiarized, or by an uncertain future the promise of which is never wholly fulfilled. Everything is viewed in the clear light of the present, with its insistent demands.

We may ask ourselves nowadays whether Austen's synthesis of the psychological and the social novel is specifically feminine, whether perhaps only a woman could have achieved it. The expression "feminine sensitivity," often used in this context, refers to a characteristic that is not so much biologically determined as culturally fostered. Little by little, something traditionally seen as a weakness came to be reinterpreted as a strength. Women realized that the domain of human relationships was one in which their social conditioning gave them the advantage over men.

We are now used to seeing the so-called soft skills, social and emotional awareness, playing a growing role in society even outside the private sphere, and becoming ever more highly valued as a result. This development began with the culture of the novel, which in its early decades was primarily a feminine culture. The novel is a school for emotional and social intelligence. For such writers as Austen, a fine ear for the undertones, nuances, and false notes in personal relationships came to be a source of literary creativeness; for their readers, this sensitivity became a positive quality in its own right and an important area of experience for them, both as individuals and in relation to society.

A new type of woman

The novel thus engendered a new self-confidence in women. Reading novels gave a woman access to experiences and insights that she could never have had within the narrow confines of her normal life. In the novel she was able to recognize her own situation and also to see her own world in a new light, as merely one among many possible others. The German philosopher Odo Marquard has used the term "pluralization of lives" to describe this phenomenon: Reading literature, and especially discussing it with other readers, broadens the scope of one's own life and affords glimpses into other modes of living of which one had previously been quite unaware.

Not that the women of the eighteenth and nineteenth centuries were enjoying a golden age of leisure and freedom in which to use their time as they chose. Whatever that commentator in *The Guardian* may have said about the amount of spare time that women had on their hands, the nurse and writer Florence Nightingale, pioneer of professional nursing care for the casualties of war, thought otherwise: "Women never have half an hour in all their lives (excepting before and after anybody is up in the house) that they can call their own, without fear of offending or of hurting some one," she wrote in her autobiographical text *Cassandra*, published in 1860. To put it slightly differently, nothing that a woman does is so important that it may not be interrupted at any moment. Caustically, Nightingale adds: "A woman cannot live in the light of intellect. Society forbids it. Those conventional frivolities, which are called her 'duties,' forbid it. Her 'domestic duties,' high-sounding words, which, for the most part, are but bad habits (which she has not the courage to enfranchise herself from, the strength to break through), forbid it." Nightingale herself exchanged the role of "angel in the house," imposed on women by the bourgeois moral code of the time, for that of an angel outside the house. She was convinced that women's passion, intellect, and need for "moral activity" could find no fulfillment in the frigid social climate of that period, in which they were kept down by the oppressive force of convention. If their spirit was not to wither away,

women had to find the courage to forsake the well-trodden ways and strike out on difficult and untried paths.

We see the middle-class women novelists of those early years—Jane Austen, the Brontë sisters, or Bettina von Arnim—engaged in a constant struggle with everyday circumstances that barely allowed them to write at all. One fundamental problem was that in the early nineteenth century almost every aspect of the life of a middle-class family took place in the single sitting-room that they shared. When the door creaked on its hinges, indicating that someone was coming in, the young Austen is reported to have hidden the manuscript on which she was working, or covered it with a sheet of blotting paper. "How she was able to effect all this," her nephew Edward writes in his memoir of her, "is surprising, for she had no separate study to repair to, and most of the work must have been done in the general sitting-room, subject to all kinds of casual interruptions."

The young, middle-class women authors of this period devoted themselves almost exclusively to novels, even if their talents might really have lain more in the direction of poetic drama or history-writing. Virginia Woolf put this down to the conditions under which the women had to write. The novel, she said—and as a novelist herself, she knew what she was talking about—was "the least concentrated form of art." A novel will tolerate its author being constantly interrupted and having to pick up the threads again later. One might say that it is the genre that is most resistant to interruption; it preserves its continuity despite pauses and distractions. Accidents, trifling events, chance encounters, unexpected opportunities—in

short, unpredictable happenings of every kind—drive the novel's plot forward and contribute to the picture it paints of the world. Moreover, the middle-class novel can tell stories that unfold very largely in parlors and drawing-rooms—in the settings, that is, where the women authors and their female readers had had their primary social experiences. Unsurprisingly, too, the characters of the protagonists are often revealed less by action than by conversation, letter-writing, and reflection. Yet even from this extremely limited repertoire of devices and locations—or perhaps because it was so very restricted—true miracles in the art of novel-writing could be produced, as Austen's *Pride and Prejudice* once again amply demonstrates.

Pride and Prejudice is a novel about choosing a partner. In accordance with the social code of the time, the sole aim of this process was to make an advantageous match. Marriage was a woman's one chance to leave home and make something of her life. But it was also a great source of difficulty and conflict since the woman was so much in the hands of other people, and it was by no means certain that their demands and expectations could be brought into line with her own wishes. At first sight, the plot of *Pride and Prejudice* seems to have been devised by a social Darwinist *avant la lettre*. The women hope to marry men who have high social status, which they, and in due course their children, will share. The men, on the other hand, compete for the prettiest women. Thanks to Darwin, we know that the males of the species see youth and beauty as indicators of reproductive fitness. The ups and downs of the courtships in the story reflect the problem of distinguishing between a passing attraction based on looks or manner, and long-term suitability—between possibly deceptive "first impressions" (the novel's original title) and what is nowadays called "forming a lasting relationship."

Yet none of this touches on the aspect of the book that still charms the reader, and that led the normally modest author to declare that her heroine, Elizabeth Bennet, was "as delightful a creature as ever appeared in print." In her, Austen created a new type of woman, the embodiment of "wit," which at that time implied agility of mind, quick understanding, and astute powers of reasoning. In this, Elizabeth is the very opposite of her mother, whom the novel portrays as a naïve and foolish proponent of the crude social-Darwinist marriage ethos of the day. What Elizabeth most detests are the attitudes and kinds of behavior that the sociologists of a later age would describe as typical of an "other-directed personality." This term is applied to individuals who allow all their decisions and actions to be prompted by influences outside themselves. Austen recognized that although in some

circumstances such a person may provide more fun, this trait will cause a woman, in particular, to form an image of herself that is based on other people's expectations. Elizabeth, by contrast, will marry, but she has made her own choice of partner, and from the very start of the relationship, she has proved her superiority where emotional and social intelligence are concerned. In addition to wit, the prerequisites for this are honesty, determination, and uncompromising realism. People with these qualities have no need to depend on others for a sense of self, but follow their own judgment and have the strength of character to revise it should that judgment prove to be an ill-founded prejudice.

Behind a pseudonym

A hundred years after Jane Austen's attempt to create a new picture of the self-determined woman of intelligence and spirit, Virginia Woolf made her famous demand for "a room of one's own" for women writers and intellectually active women in general. To ensure that works written by women were no longer primarily exposures of their own sufferings and "the dumping-ground for the personal emotions," the conditions of production needed to be changed. Financial freedom and time and a space of one's own were, Woolf argued, the necessary foundations for the writing of independent, autonomous works of literature. Men, hitherto accustomed to being waited on as masters of the household, would surely be prepared to meet women on their own terms once women had demonstrated independent control of their own time and working-space. Then, but only then, could men and women engage in "the most interesting, exciting and important conversation that has ever been heard."

What was new about this demand was that it was now being aired in the public arena and had become something of a political issue. It had already been articulated, if only in private correspondence, by the American writer Harriet Beecher Stowe, who gained international celebrity with her novel *Uncle Tom's Cabin.* "If I am to write, I must have a room to myself, which shall be *my* room," she had written to her husband. Like many of her fellow women authors, she had discovered her desire to write and her talent at an early age, and she had won first prize in a story-writing competition at the age of twenty-two. But instead of making a career of her writing, she married a man who, like her father and her six brothers, was a theologian. Unlike the four great English women authors of the nineteenth century—Jane Austen, Emily Brontë, Charlotte Brontë, and George Eliot, not one of whom had any children, and two of whom never married—Stowe had seven children.

"All last winter I felt the need of some place where I could go and be quiet and satisfied," she wrote to her husband. "Our children are just coming to the age when everything depends on my efforts. They ... need a mother's whole attention. Can I lawfully divide my attention by literary efforts?" By the time she had attended to the children's lessons, taken care of the little ones, bought food, mended clothes, and darned socks, she was too tired, she said, to sit down and write for a newspaper, even though the Stowes needed whatever money she could earn. It was only rarely during the years of bringing up and educating the children that she managed to do any writing.

Typical of the obstacles that women writers had to overcome, in both the public and the private sphere, is an incident described by the French author George Sand. After nine years of an oppressive marriage, she left her husband and started working on a book. Her mother-in-law promptly took her to task. Was it true that she proposed to publish books? What a peculiar idea! She just hoped that she did not intend to put her name—her husband's name—on the covers! And so Aurore Dudevant, *née* Dupin, embarked on her literary career under a pseudonym, circumspectly choosing a male first name. She was not the only woman of her day to gain an entreé to the male world of literature by pretending that her manuscripts were the work of a man. All three Brontë sisters published their works under male pseudonyms, calling themselves Currer (Charlotte), Ellis (Emily), and Acton (Anne) Bell. At one point, through an unfortunate series of misunderstandings, at least one of their publishers learned that the three supposedly male authors were actually women, and there was some danger of the Brontës' true identities becoming known. Emily, whose one novel, *Wuthering Heights*, had been rejected by the contemporary public as tasteless and incomprehensible, was particularly insistent that the sisters keep the protection that their pseudonyms afforded them.

George Eliot—whose real name was Mary Ann Evans and who called herself Marianne or Marian in private—published her early reviews, essays, and translations anonymously, including her translation of Ludwig Feuerbach's *Das Wesen des Christentums* (*The Essence of Christianity*), and then used her male pen name for her novels. Unlike the Brontë sisters, she chose to reveal her identity as a woman herself, in a letter to *The Times*. What prompted her to do so was a press campaign that attributed her novels to a baker's son, who was delighted with his sudden fame. Evans was "living in sin" with a married man, George Henry Lewes, himself a writer and the father of three boys. She adopted his first name and added a common English surname made up of five letters, like the name of the man she loved. Her reason, as Lewes explained in a letter, had not been fear for her reputation in so-called "good society"; rather, she was concerned to ensure that her book should be judged on its own merits, and not be condemned a priori as the work of a woman, or of a particular woman—that is, a woman who was not invited anywhere because her way of life offended against the morality of Victorian society. Even after Evans had revealed her true identity, she continued to publish under the name George Eliot. A rival who knew her as Marian from her early life later wrote that Eliot had been a woman made by her own

she wrote her first novel, *Claudine at School*, which presented a new, contemporary, refreshing type of young woman, a sort of alter ego of Colette herself, her husband published it under his own name. The book was a bestseller, and Willy bathed in public acclaim as "Claudine's papa" (thus making himself intellectually the father of his own wife), while locking Colette in a study to write more "Claudine" novels. Six years later, she left him.

Children or books

That men should make a profession out of their impulse to write was socially acceptable. For a very long time, women with the same ambition would receive the sort of advice that a (male) novelist gave Aurore Dudevant (*née* Dupin) even before she had transformed herself into George Sand: "To be frank, a woman ought not to write ... Take my advice: don't write books, have children."

Aut liberi aut libri—either children or books. Until printing was invented, it was the rule in the Christian Middle Ages that anyone who wanted to read, let alone write (which in most cases meant no more than copying), had to enter a monastery or convent, because it was there that written matter was to be found and there that it was considered to belong. With the rise of female literacy, that proverbial saying, which was originally aimed at monks, was an obvious tool to use against women's nascent desire to become writers. Male condemnation of women writers—at a later date, Friedrich Nietzsche spitefully referred to them as "literary females"—always followed this

hands, who never for a moment forgot the identity that she had created for herself.

Jane Austen, on the other hand, took care to remain anonymous for as long as she lived. The title pages of her books indicated only that they were "By a Lady." Evidently she wanted the reading public to know that *Sense and Sensibility* or *Pride and Prejudice* had been written by a woman, but she chose to leave her readers in the dark about her identity. Austen's invisibility gave her a certain freedom of action, though for the most part only on paper—only metaphorically, as it were—and at the price of living in obscurity. When she received a late proposal of marriage, she declined it after lengthy deliberation.

A further variation on this theme concerns men—usually husbands—who claim to have authored work actually written by a woman. This claim may have been made with or without the woman's consent. Probably the most notorious example is that of the French writer Colette, whose first marriage was to a man fourteen years her senior, the critic, writer, and publisher's son Henry Gauthier-Villars, known as Willy. When "either–or" pattern that categorically excluded any third way, even if it was a compromise. The requirement to choose one and thereby necessarily forgo the other was tied, moreover, to an image of woman that obliged her always to choose the first option: If she did not, she was considered to be going against her nature.

The idea that men and women by their nature belong to different orders, and that the mixing of roles represents a threat to both sexes, persisted stubbornly throughout the Victorian era and well into the twentieth century (indeed, it lingers on even today). It was still there, for example, when the Beat generation was seeking an alternative way of life defined by the search for intense experiences, in contrast to conventional notions of a settled home and regular work. In Jack Kerouac's celebrated novel of 1957, it is only men, in fact only young men, who are "on the road." The writer Joyce Johnson, who was Kerouac's partner for a while when she was young, wanted to go with him on his travels and saw no reason why she should not do so. But, as she recalled thirty years later, whenever she raised the subject, Kerouac would interrupt her, saying that, like all women, what she really wanted was children. Even more than to be a great writer, she longed (according to him) to bring new life into the world. Johnson, however, saw that option as being just another link in the long chain of suffering and death.

In her day, George Sand was already adept at turning such dubious advice against the men giving it. She supposedly burst out laughing and replied, "My dear sir, pray follow this prescription yourself!" It is not recorded whether the gentle-man in question truly understood what was being asked of him—to bring forth children, not books. Although it is not granted to them to bear children, men do at least insist on their privilege of producing books. Women who write are dangerous and live dangerously partly because they challenge the male prerogative of creativity, turning on its head the traditional division of labor between the sexes, according to which the man actively engenders and produces while the woman passively receives and bears children.

Among the medieval saints' lives there are stories of women who disguised themselves as monks and thereby achieved both sanctity and an enhanced status in society. By putting on the monk's habit, they gained in social mobility, albeit at the cost of renouncing both their femininity and their sexuality. Centuries later, when such women as George Sand not only published under male pseudonyms but also wore male costume in public and disguised their true sex, they too were concerned to increase their freedom of movement, not least in a purely practical sense: Women's clothing tended to be an encumbrance on dirty pavements; it was difficult to make headway; and good dresses were quickly ruined. Male dress, besides being far more convenient, also gave them access to establishments to which women were not admitted. In such situations, it was essential to have the kind of poise that we would nowadays call "cool," the trick of wearing men's clothes with studied nonchalance, as though it came naturally. By the age of seventeen, Aurore Dupin, who had been taken out of school and enjoyed a largely unrestricted life in the country with her grand-mother, had managed to acquire the necessary ease of manner in the course of long rides and walks. To an old schoolfriend enthusing about her first balls (at that time the social arena in which the first steps toward a possible marriage could be taken under a watchful parental eye), she wrote back: "But you don't go out in a full-length man's coat and a cap, with a gun over your shoulder, to roam across ploughed fields ..." Thus began a life that flouted convention in every way. After she had more or less established herself in society as a writer and also seduced many, mostly younger, men, among them some of great eminence, Sand gave up wearing male clothing, except every now and again for amusement, simply to scandalize people. She found new ways to conduct her life and to climb the social ladder without renouncing her femininity and sexuality: On the contrary, she made use of both in the service of her freedom. This brought her accusations of hypocrisy. Charles Baudelaire reviled her as the smugly respectable face of immorality ("le Prudhomme de l'immoralité"). Simone de Beauvoir castigated her for putting on a mask of virtue to give her opportunistic behavior a veneer of moral respectability. But perhaps when Sand proclaimed her love of truth, this was a coded reference to her determination to remain true to *herself*—not to be conventionally moral but to assert and express her true nature.

All of these were early, sometimes hesitant, attempts to bridge the gulf between the male and female spheres, often with the aim of extending a woman's freedom of activity, but in some cases simply in order to earn a living. In the nineteenth century, it was not uncommon for women to dress as men when looking for work, even enlisting as soldiers just as impoverished men did. And time and again women have refused to forgo books for the sake of children, or children for the sake of books, but have chosen both—if they were fortunate enough to be able to choose. Sand herself had two children whom she took back into her care after her first literary successes, and they naturally went with her when she spent the winter with Frédéric Chopin in Majorca.

The consequence for such women was a life that was split in two and often deeply troubled. Typically, it might follow this pattern: first attempts at writing as a young woman, usually without publishing anything; then marriage, babies, bringing up children; writing, if at all, in between changing diapers or at night, often with pangs of conscience. Later, if the marriage survived (which it often did not, because the husband could not come to terms with his wife's unconventional lifestyle), the woman might have a career as a writer in her remaining years—although even if she lived to enjoy it, that final phase of life was not as long as it generally is today. Bettina von Arnim was one writer whose life followed the pattern: At the age of fifty, after twenty years of married life and maternal duties (the children were beyond their neediest phase, and her husband had died a few days before his fiftieth birthday), she embarked on a new life as a successful author.

The twentieth century offered somewhat more favorable conditions for combining children with a writing career. This resulted in part from advances in social welfare and technology, and in part from the professionalization of writing as publishing adapted itself to the modern business

An original manuscript page
by George Sand

world. The French author Florence Montreynaud, who wrote a major work, *The Twentieth Century of Women*, in the 1980s at the same time as bringing up four children, expressly made *et liberi et libri*—"both children and books"—her personal motto. In this, she was following the example of such writers as the Swedish children's author Astrid Lindgren and the African American Nobel Prize-winner Toni Morrison, who were both not only mothers but also combined their writing with jobs as publisher's readers. Lindgren had shown that efficient organization of one's daily life was essential if one was to unite the two worlds; nowadays women are bombarded with advice on this topic.

Morrison went so far as to say that looking after her children enabled her to get rid of useless ballast in her life. Being interrupted by her children and being there for them, she has explained, were not necessarily detrimental to her writing: It was a matter of concentration. While the children were still small, she decided to give up the habit of going off to a special room to write because then the children, feeling abandoned, would immediately come and disturb her, and she would be split between being a mother and being a writer. Instead, she moved her work into the living-room—back, in fact, to where women's novel-writing had begun. The children demanded things that no one else had ever expected of her: being a good manager, having a sense of humor, fetching whatever someone happened to need. Morrison could be herself. Her children seemed to want the person in her that she liked best. If being a writer means speaking as one person to others, why should it be possible to produce works only in self-imposed isolation, and not among people?

By contrast, Simone de Beauvoir's fierce call to abolish the myth of motherhood, which she voiced in the early 1970s in a dialogue with the American feminist Betty Friedan, seems illiberal and remote from the mundane matters that real women are confronted with in their everyday lives: "No woman should be allowed to stay at home to raise her children. Women should not have the choice, because if there is a choice, too many women will make that one." Once again someone is laying down the law about what women should or should not do, and this time it is a woman who saw herself as being in the vanguard of the movement for female emancipation.

The art of living

To return once more to Jane Austen. In her last novel, *Persuasion*, we find this moving description of Anne Elliot: "She had been forced into prudence in her youth, she learned romance as she grew older—the natural sequel of an unnatural beginning." This comment was equally true of the author, who might be called a late developer. One year after completing *Persuasion*, she died, at the age of forty-one, when "she was just beginning to

GEORGE ELIOT (1819–1880)
Sketch by Samuel Laurence (1812–1884), 1860
Private collection

feel confidence in her own success," as her nephew noted in his memoir of her. Had she lived a few years longer, Virginia Woolf has suggested, Austen would have emerged from the obscurity in which she lived: "She would have stayed in London, dined out, lunched out, met famous people, made new friends, read, travelled, and carried back to the quiet country cottage a hoard of observations to feast upon at leisure." In a nutshell, she would have had a little more from life than simply her writing, which has principally given her a posthumous life. And she would surely have written other novels, different novels, and would have developed new techniques to do even greater justice to the complexity of human nature that she understood more fully the longer she lived.

Woolf's reflections are more than mere idle speculation, for they describe the sense of unfinished business that we often feel when we contemplate the lives of Austen and her fellow women authors. Very few of them died having had all they wanted out of life: Life had not brought them, by the end of their days, the fulfillment that it might have offered.

Yet it does not have to be like this. Perhaps, as Woolf suggested, a few additional years would have made all the difference. Since Austen's time, life expectancy has increased by forty years or so, and it is still increasing, thereby making possible developmental processes that require more time because they involve following byways and indirect routes, perhaps even losing the way at times. A person whose early years are unhappy, or not "normal," or are even lived too prudently, needs time to change course; ingrained patterns of behavior seldom vanish with a sudden blaze of

revelation. A life such as George Sand's, which lasted for more than seventy years, shows how much even a nineteenth-century woman could achieve and experience. To have more years of life is a great advantage when it comes to developing the art of living, which could be said to consist of discovering by trial and error what is most appropriate to one's own nature. "Why can't I try on different lives, like dresses, to see which fits best and is most becoming?" Sylvia Plath asked in her journal. Yet after the separation from her husband, the poet Ted Hughes, who loved another woman, she did not start a new life in London with her two small children, as she had said she would, but instead chose to die. "The worst thing that can happen to a woman is her first husband," Colette's mother, Sido, is said to have prophesied to her daughter.

The "room of one's own" that Virginia Woolf so insistently demanded in the name of women writers and of art is an existential metaphor for a life of one's own, under one's own control. Such a life is not one of considering, sorting, and choosing options from what is available: It is more like a battle. That the art of living is more in need of the skills of a wrestler than those of a dancer was noted even in Classical times by the emperor and philosopher Marcus Aurelius in his *Meditations*. The attempt to master it only rarely results in an ideal, harmonious life, a life resembling a work of art. Generally, what is achieved is only an imperfect, fragmentary existence full of setbacks and new starts; a person grapples with life under conditions that are often neither congenial nor predictable, that she or he has not chosen and cannot control. Novels show us how lives can be led under such circumstances—another reason, perhaps, why the novel is the genre most favored by women.

The struggle for authenticity

In the twentieth century, women began to liberate themselves from the narrow confines of the middle-class living-room and to conduct their lives a little more in the way that Virginia Woolf wished Jane Austen could have done, the way that she managed for herself, despite the added problem of her psychological instability. And yet the lives of these modern women continued to be dominated by the struggle against convention and for authenticity, especially as far as their writing, the very heart of their lives, was concerned. The independent woman author—independent not only financially but also in the sense of the maxim that Oscar Wilde said should be written over the portal of the new world, "Be thyself"—this economically and existentially independent woman, whose writing is anchored in her own life and simultaneously transcends it, still represents a highly attractive model of an authentic life for a woman.

But what *is* an authentic life and, more specifically, an authentic life for a woman? From a host of biographies we know that the quest for authenticity is essentially a struggle against being embroiled in whatever is inauthentic. That statement may seem to explain an enigmatic term simply by using its equally enigmatic negative. If we are to believe the French author Nathalie Sarraute, "what is nowadays called the inauthentic" was discovered by Gustave Flaubert, who showed it to us in his novel *Madame Bovary* (1857). Everyone, Sarraute says, remembers that deceptive world: "The world that Madame Bovary sees, all the desires, ideas, and dreams by which she tries to shape her life are inspired by a series of images derived from the most debased forms of Romanticism. We remember the young girl's daydreaming, her marriage, her yearning for luxury, her notions of the life led by the rich and powerful ... all the roles that she is constantly playing—all of that is rooted in the most banal conventions."

This condescending and contemptuous characterization of Emma Bovary surely does her an injustice, for she also has qualities that transcend trivial conventionality: courage, imagination, an urgency of desire, and a hunger for life. Has she—an enthusiastic and sensitive reader—simply read the wrong books? It was the nineteenth-century German writer Wilhelm Hauff who quipped that the company of bad books is often more dangerous than that of bad people. The novel that provides Emma with her sweetest reveries is Jacques-Henri Bernardin de Saint-Pierre's tale of love in an exotic setting, *Paul et Virginie* (1788), in which feminine sensitivity is celebrated and, in accordance with the ideas of the philosopher Jean-Jacques Rousseau, the enticements of civilization have disastrous consequences. With its blend of sentimentalism and exoticism, and its emphasis on harmony and conciliation, this novel may already have been regarded as kitsch by the middle of the nineteenth century. Apart from this, Emma's reading includes sentimental popular novels and the historical novels of Sir Walter Scott. They all

arouse in her a longing for something unattainable and a sense of her own inadequacy. Would she have fared differently if she had read Austen's *Pride and Prejudice*, or indeed Flaubert's *Madame Bovary*? Certainly she would have acquired sounder critical judgment and been better able to appraise her own day-to-day world. But what Flaubert chiefly wanted to show us through the figure of Emma Bovary is what he regarded as a wrong relationship to reading and to art in general. The happiness she derives from her reading makes Emma conscious of the misery of her daily life. That in itself is reasonable, but it also devalues her everyday life, making it seem trivial and vulgar. Emma begins to measure her life against the pictures in her imagination, and rejects it as inauthentic.

It is significant that the full title of Flaubert's novel is *Madame Bovary. Patterns of Provincial Life*. Emma is a provincial, a country girl. But the rural world is far from being the quintessence of unspoilt existence that was evoked in *Paul et Virginie*. Here "provincial" signifies everything that prevents one from living an authentic, autonomous life, and Emma cannot manage to shake off the influence of this provincialism. The provinces do not relax their grip on her. She pursues a dream of art and, in so doing, wrecks her life. It is this form of falsehood—art as a substitute for life—and not literature (or indeed women) as such that Flaubert calls to account in *Madame Bovary*. When he brings about his heroine's death, he is killing off a part of himself, his own sentimental past, by exposing and exorcising it in the novel. (Goethe had similarly inflicted his own sufferings on Werther and then let him

die, thereby distancing himself as an author from the figure who was based on himself.)

At the same time, Flaubert demonstrates the sovereign means of escape from the banal conventions of daily existence, the commonplaces and clichés—in a word, the inauthentic—namely, by creating art, the greatest possible art. How can one liberate oneself from the banality of convention, from kitsch and vulgarity, from the provincial, from the influence of bad books? By writing a *good* book, one that is neither banal nor conventional in its style and its aspirations, however banal and conventional the characters may show themselves to be in the course of the plot. Flaubert took this path with *Madame Bovary*. And many modern authors, including a large number of women, have followed in his footsteps.

So far we have been looking mainly at the social and family roles of women writers, and the limitations that these roles impose on them. Individuals who can achieve their aims only while keeping out of the public eye, and who find themselves in irreconcilable opposition to their society, are living dangerously. But so also are

An original manuscript page
by Simone de Beauvoir

those who are inwardly at odds with themselves and thereby condemned to a continual struggle. Inner conflicts of this kind are, for example, the states of confusion and hesitation between concession and rebellion, compliance and resistance, that are so graphically depicted in novels from *Clarissa* and *Werther* onward. People trying to break free from constraints, especially inner constraints, will inevitably inflict psychological damage on themselves and on those around them—the price of gaining a greater measure of self-determination.

Lady Lazarus

A prime example of a modern woman author plagued by inner conflicts, who was brought down not so much by social pressures as by her own uncompromising quest for authenticity, is Sylvia Plath. She showed extraordinary promise as a girl and gained recognition, in the form of awards and publication, at a young age. Her

relatively small body of work—poetry above all, a few stories, an autobiographical novel that appeared shortly before her suicide at the age of thirty, and of course her journals—can be seen as confessional writing, revealing the dark side of existence. Even if, like Emma Bovary, Plath came from a provincial background (in her case, the suburban United States), her drama was not one of social conditions, narrowness of milieu, or a lack of recognition by society. Nor, however, was it only a drama of relationships, as her (psychoanalytically aware) fans were quick to assume, making her into a feminist literary icon. Plath's drama cannot be explained solely by the early death of her father, an ambivalent mother fixation, and a poet husband who deserted her, leaving her with two small children. It was, more than anything, the drama of her sense of herself as a writer; her husband, Ted Hughes, acknowledged this, even if there is an element of retrospective idealization in his assessment of her. Some years after Plath's death, he wrote in his foreword to her journals, when they were published: "There was something about her reminiscent of what one reads of Islamic fanatic lovers of God—a craving to strip away everything from some ultimate intensity, some communion with spirit, or with reality, or simply with intensity itself. She showed something violent in this, something very primitive, perhaps very female, a readiness, even a need, to sacrifice everything to the new birth."

If Hughes is to be believed (and the journals confirm this interpretation), then what constituted Plath's existential drama, the drama of her consciousness, was her struggle to break through to her true, authentic self by casting off all the other, lesser, inauthentic selves that were embodied, for example, in her relationships with her mother and brother and even her husband and children. The medium through which she tried to achieve this breakthrough was of course her writing. Behind the façade of everyday living a sacred drama of poetic transfiguration was being played out, driven by Plath's fear of becoming submerged in the banality of convention and stereotyped roles and consequently failing as a poet. Her writing became nothing less than an anticipation and celebration of her own dying for the sake of the paradise of poetry. "I desire the things that will destroy me in the end," Plath writes in her journal as early as 1950. And in one of her most famous poems she appears as "Lady Lazarus": "Dying/ Is an art, like everything else./ I do it exceptionally well." The climax of this deliberately shocking poem, which celebrates a kind of psychoanalytical exorcism, is a concentration-camp striptease in which the "I" of the poem melts and fuses with the enemy, and finally rises like a phoenix "out of the ash" to "eat men like air."

The struggle for authenticity has something decidedly violent about it. In his famous work *Sincerity and Authenticity* (1972), the great American literary critic and cultural commentator Lionel Trilling reminds us how central the idea of violence is to the meaning of the word "authentic" in its Greek derivation: "*Authenteo*: to have full power over; also, to commit a murder. *Authentes*: not only a master and a doer, but also a perpetrator, a murderer, even a self-murderer, a suicide." These "ancient and forgotten denotations,"

according to Trilling, tell us a great deal about the nature and intention of "modern" (that is, early twentieth-century) art and its aspiration to authenticity. Accustomed as we now are, he says, to the radicalism of that art, seeing it from our vantage point of some decades later, we have forgotten how much ruthlessness was required at the time to produce art that broke all the rules that up to then had been inviolable; but also "how extreme an exercise of personal will was needed to overcome the sentiment of non-being."

Perhaps that was Plath's real drama: that even when she had escaped from that feeling of "non-being"—anonymity, insignificance, worthlessness, but also lethargy and weakness of will—she was still in constant fear of relapsing into it. The terrible sense of her own limitations and emptiness made her seek refuge in the conviction that art was the way to conquer that condition. There were moments when, in the intoxication of creativity, she succeeded; but the *horror vacui* was never staved off for long. Plath was terrified of her inner void, and needed writing to fill it. And so every period in her life when she was prevented from writing either by everyday commitments or by an inner paralysis seemed to her to be so much life wasted, and this exacerbated her lack of self-esteem. "Writing is a religious act," she wrote in her journal; Hughes shared that view and no doubt reinforced her belief in it. He always stressed the closeness of poetry to shamanism and to Islamic mysticism. In this connection he, too, gives images of violence, such as beasts of prey, a central role in his poems. In Plath's poetry, however, the use of violent images has clearly Christian overtones and is increasingly

directed against her own self and her own body. Plath noted that writing was the heaviest responsibility in the world; "you are crucified by your own limitations." The longed-for release from these limitations and the breakthrough to authentic experience could be found only in the stormy heights of poetry, but even this could not keep the bell jar—Plath's image for the symbolic death she experienced in everyday life, and the title she gave to her only novel—permanently lifted. Writing continued to be a storm under the bell jar. There Plath sat, "stewing in my own sour air," as she puts it in her novel. That is what destroyed her.

The fight with the Angel

For Virginia Woolf, too, when she demanded privacy and material independence for women writers, more was at stake than just writing. Art had to be produced that was not trivial or conventional, not merely naturalistic in its depiction of life, but that convinced the reader that "this is the truth." Woolf's reflections focused less, however, on a woman author's authenticity and more on her integrity and that of her work. "Authenticity" signifies genuineness, certified authorship, and also true, autonomous self-expression. If being authentic meant being resistant to all outside influence, then there would be no authentic individuals. We would not even be able to read anything, for whenever we read a piece of literature, we voluntarily submit ourselves to the views of another person. And there would be no writers either, because no one writes entirely from the resources of his or her own personality. Every writer has first been a reader. And if being authentic meant living entirely according to rules of one's own making, and ultimately being one's own creation and living one's life as a sort of myth, that would be sheer hubris. We do not owe our own existence and circumstances to ourselves. Whatever adjustments we make inevitably have the character of afterthoughts and temporary arrangements—and in most cases, we cannot even foresee the consequences.

We and our works can, however, possess integrity, not just in a moral but also in an aesthetic and existential sense. Integrity means incorruptibility and a certain wholeness or invulnerability. To live truly *authentically*, one would have to be God; but for integrity, ordinary human conditions (and the contradictions implicit in them), together with strength of will, are enough.

Woolf regarded integrity as the writer's backbone. An author who does not pay her bills or her taxes may be a bad citizen, but she can still be a good writer. Being *unable* to pay may dull her perceptions as a writer, however, because her resentment or outrage at her poverty may rob her of the sense of what is right or wrong for her work, and also deprive her of the energy to maintain herself at the peak of her art. If a woman writer is conscious that the people in her immediate circle consider what she does to be inappropriate and unimportant on the grounds that she is a woman and that women should have other priorities than writing books, not only does this damage her psychologically, but also her work may suffer. We sense her anger in its lack of moderation, her fear in its imprecision, her bitterness in its polemical tone. Thus integrity is another name for that manner of mastering life that we encountered in Jane Austen's novels, where the essential qualities were honesty, firmness of resolve, and wit.

Integrity depends on the ability to ignore one's own physical and mental state and not to make it (as Plath did) the key to everything one says or writes. But for this to be possible, certain material, social, mental, and psychological conditions have to be met. Woolf repeatedly pointed out that the poetic spirit is not like the wind that "bloweth where it listeth," but that certain requirements, not least material ones, must be fulfilled in order to create the intellectual freedom that gives rise to great literary works. Writers should not be enmeshed in bitterness and anger, but should be able to write as free spirits, which implies standing back from oneself. There are some basic conditions without which that detachment cannot be achieved. Hunger, external pressures, and inner obsessions are not helpful. Yet equally unhelpful is total freedom from the constraints that give a spur to the artist's will. The pleasure principle, the enjoyment of a comfortable state in which the self has total power and autonomy, is not necessarily conducive to producing literature.

For this ambivalent relationship between constraint and freedom in the creative process, Woolf devised a powerful and evocative metaphor: the struggle with the "Angel in the House." She spoke about it in a lecture on "Professions for Women" that she delivered in 1931, a few days before her forty-ninth birthday, to the Women's Service League in London. Her subject was nothing less than her own most significant professional experiences: how she had become a writer, what obstacles she had faced, and with what resources she had been able to overcome them. Woolf refers to some English women writers, among them Jane Austen and George Eliot. "Many famous women, and many more unknown and forgotten," she says, had smoothed the path for her and directed her steps. A woman writer in the early twentieth century was no longer a pioneer: "When I came to write, there were very few material obstacles in my way. Writing was a reputable and harmless occupation," at least for a young woman of good family. "The family peace was not broken by the scratching of a pen. No demand was made upon the family purse." On the contrary, by reviewing books, Woolf could even earn a little money. So had she any experiences worth passing on to her audience—or had other writers already dealt with the significant issues and passed on their insights long before, so that she needed only to follow in their footsteps?

The picture was not as idyllic as it might seem. For scarcely had Woolf taken up her pen when a phantom appeared. It bothered her, wasted her time, tormented her. She had made every effort, she declared, to kill it. Countless times she had picked up her inkpot and thrown it at the phantom, which would thrust itself between her and the paper when she was writing her reviews. The creature's fictitious nature gave it a great advantage: "It is far harder to kill a phantom than a reality." It kept creeping back into Woolf's consciousness when she thought she had finished it off. At last she had managed to do away with it once and for all. Had she been brought to court, she would have pleaded self-defense, for if she had not killed it, it would have killed her: "Killing the Angel in the House was part of the occupation of a woman writer." Writing and life, says Woolf, most resemble each other in that both are a battle against illusions, and this life-or-death struggle only ever has one victor.

Who is this Angel in the House? Not a man, but a woman who gives expression to a man's attitudes. Let us hear what she has to say. She says: Become like me—immensely charming, sympathetic, utterly unselfish, self-sacrificing, conciliatory. All entirely the wrong qualities for a writer, in Woolf's opinion. To us nowadays the Angel in the House sounds like a legacy from earlier times, when there were songs extolling the blessings of married love and pictures of good housewives with titles that included that phrase. In Woolf's own words, the Angel is "the ideal of womanhood created by the imaginations of men and women at a certain stage in their pilgrimage." With her eye still on Victorian constraints on women, Woolf did not take into account here that the angel who comes between author and work might have other faces than that of the Angel in the House—it might be an angel of violence, of death, or of utopian visions—and that not every angel can be wrestled with and defeated in the same way.

Can we say today that the Angel in the House, at least, has been defeated? Leaving aside the various reservations that come to mind, let us say "yes." Yet even for Virginia Woolf, more than seventy years ago, disposing of that particular enemy was only one step along the way, and she could not, and would not, stop there. Is it really the case, her train of thought continues, that the young woman writer—once she has rid herself of the falsehood that the Angel expects of her—only has to be herself? "Ah, but what is 'herself'? I mean, what is a woman?" Overcoming the traditional image of a woman is no more than the first milestone in a woman author's struggle for her integrity. The second is to be able to speak openly about her own passions or, in Woolf's words, to tell the truth about her "own experiences as a body." Woolf did not feel that the pilgrimage of men and women had yet reached that point. In this respect, too, we appear to have made some progress. In the last seventy years we have seen a series of female D.H. Lawrences. Some have even been able to charge convention head-on without doing such catastrophic damage to their imagination as the authors of *Lady Chatterley's Lover* and *The Bell Jar.*

This leaves one other problem, which Woolf addresses only indirectly. To put it in old-fashioned terms, men who write have muses to inspire them. These are normally women. But who are the muses for women who write? Men? And are there any men as yet—are there any men at all—who are willing and able to assume this role, which might be of crucial importance for the future of literature? The future of fiction, so Woolf believed, depended very much on the extent to which "men can be educated to stand free speech in a woman." And to the question of what sort of men these would be, her answer was "men with whom a woman can live in perfect freedom, without any fear."

The Map of Love

THE ANCESTORS OF WOMEN WHO WRITE

It would not be true to say that women were continuously oppressed and discriminated against, with no voices raised in dissent, until suddenly—at the time of the French Revolution, say—at last there was a change for the better. Even Simone de Beauvoir, who pointed out that the history of women had always been made by men, admitted that some periods (for example, long stretches of the eighteenth century) had been particularly favorable to women.

Ever since the late Middle Ages, some women and some men had opposed the disparagement of women and denied that they lacked intellectual powers. In the fifteenth century, the figure of the "ladies' champion" appears, writing in praise of women, and some two hundred years later, we find men who are outright feminists, arguing

that women should not be judged by what they have achieved in the past, since after all they have generally been denied the opportunity—that is, the freedom or the education—to fulfill their potential.

One of the most widely read literary works of the late Middle Ages was the thirteenth-century *Roman de la rose*. It was originally written as an allegory of courtly love, but a later continuation offered a critique of contemporary society and culture. It denounced women as worthless creatures and provided men with a stock of accusations to use against them, such as "All of you are, will be, or have been whores, whether in fact or only in your desires." The *Roman de la rose* gave rise to a Europe-wide controversy about the sexes, the so-called *querelle des femmes*. It was a woman, Christine de Pisan (1364–c. 1430), who supplied the crucial arguments against the long tradition of discrimination against women reaching back to antiquity. She pointed out that it was not women who had written the books and recorded the evidence that was used against them. Women knew very well that the accusations were false; if they had written the books themselves, the picture would be very different. Christine de Pisan was one of the first to invoke the authority of her own experience as a woman: Since she was "really and truly" of the female sex, she claimed she was "more entitled" to speak on the subject "than someone who lacks that experience" and talks nonsense based on supposition and hearsay.

In her *Book of the City of Ladies* (1405), Pisan went still further, critically reviewing the prevailing canon of virtues and models of behavior.

She examined misogynistic stereotypes, picked them apart, and refuted them, substituting each time a contrasting example of a great woman. In this way, she created an alternative genealogy for women to claim and to cite in their defense.

In a certain sense, the present book is a continuation of Pisan's idea of a virtual city of women. It is a gallery and a refuge, made up of the stories of women whose urge to be writers drove them to opt for a dangerous life.

HILDEGARD OF BINGEN

*H*ildegard was forty-two years old before she started to write. She had experienced visions even as a small child, but now "a fiery light with flashes of lightning" came down "from a clear sky," and "suddenly the meaning of the Scriptures, of the Psalter, the Gospels, and the other Catholic books of the Old and the New Testament" was revealed to her. Hildegard was called to be a prophetess. Out of the radiance a heavenly voice spoke to her, saying, "Frail woman ... say and write all that you see and hear!" Hildegard was reluctant, however, for according to the teachings of St. Paul, a woman was forbidden to preach, write, or speak in public. But then she suffered an illness, which she interpreted as divine punishment: "Then at last, defeated by all my suffering, I began to write." And her health was restored. It was some years later, when Pope Eugenius III visited Trier, that Hildegard's prophetic gift was recognized and, as part of that recognition, her writing was sanctioned.

Besides the *Scivias*, a cosmological interpretation of salvational history (the course of events leading to the redemption of humankind), Hildegard wrote treatises on medicine, morals, and man's place in creation. She regarded herself as a prophetess, for at that time receiving instruction through visions was the only way that a woman could study theology. She did not challenge the social hierarchy or the relative status of the sexes, which were "ordained by God." Yet there was a very earthly aspect to her vocation to become a writer, for the true cause of her illness was surely the stress induced by the prohibition on writing, and when this was removed, she regained her health. In the seclusion of her convent in Bingen, writing, as the expression of an inner voice—in Hildegard's case, the divine voice—became the means through which a new female sense of self found expression. Hildegard wrote that she flattered no one and spoke without duplicity. She was as solid as a rock and would not yield to anyone. She had a child's simplicity: She spoke of nothing but what she knew and saw.

HILDEGARD OF BINGEN
Postcard, *c.* 1910
In Hildegard's case, writing meant dictating, unless perhaps she made a first draft on a wax tablet.
A scribe then transferred the text to parchment, tacitly editing it and correcting the Latin
grammar. The abbot had assigned an assistant to Hildegard for this purpose: first, from 1141 to 1173,
a monk named Volmar, and after his death, another called Wibert. The third and final stage was
the preparation of the fair copy, which survives in its manuscript form to this day.

CHRISTINE DE PISAN
Illumination from *Collected Works
of Christine de Pisan*, 1410–11
British Library, London

CHRISTINE DE PISAN

With Christine de Pisan, a completely new type of woman appeared on the scene: the professional woman writer, supporting herself through her work as a secular author. Pisan was impelled toward the "sweet pleasure of knowledge and learning," of writing and publishing, by the independent but precarious situation in which she found herself after the death of her husband. Deprived of male protection, she took the masculine role upon herself, refloated the ship of life through her own efforts, and steered it, with herself and her daughters on board, through the deep waters of this earthly existence. Christine de Pisan, who began as a copyist and then worked as an author running her own scriptorium, is rightly seen as the forerunner of all women who are active in the world of books today, from writers to publishers.

In her books, Christine de Pisan urged sexual restraint on women and encouraged them to turn away from love as a passion. She was not the only woman writer throughout history to offer this kind of advice. Such views did not, however, stem from prudery, as men were quick to insinuate. It was rather that these women were anxious to avoid the claim to ownership that men made over their bodies and, above all, their lives. Dear ladies, Christine urges them, always consider how men accuse you of weakness and moral laxity, and yet at the same time what efforts they make to catch you in their toils. "Flee, flee, dear ladies," from men's immoderate and foolish demands for love, for it will be you who pay the price in the end.

MADELEINE DE SCUDÉRY

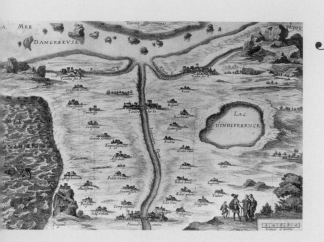

Above: "Carte de tendre" from *Clélie, histoire romaine*, 1654

MADELEINE DE SCUDÉRY
Painting by an unknown French artist,
seventeenth century
Bibliothèque Marguerite Durand, Paris

Nowadays the works of Madeleine de Scudéry are remembered chiefly by literary historians, consisting as they do of lengthy heroic romances and a small number of poems. What has become proverbial, however, is the "Carte de tendre," the map of tender love, that Scudéry had bound into the first volume of her novel *Clélie, histoire romaine* (1654). It is an allegorical map of the broad terrain of love, and it is no accident that it is reminiscent of a game board. It represents a new, feminine code of behavior in love, in which sensual passion is transcended by a sympathy between souls. The map guides the inexperienced lover along the dangerous path, hemmed in on the left by the Sea of Enmity and on the right by the Lake of Indifference, toward the three possible kinds of love: love as respect, as high esteem, and as affection. The last of these, the most desirable of the three, may be reached directly via the River of Affection, which runs through the middle of the map. Beyond the City of Tender Love, the river flows into the perilous sea, on the far side of which lie the as-yet-unknown provinces of love.

At the same time as women were making determined efforts to gain entry to the traditionally male-dominated realm of literature, they were also attempting to replace the male idea of love—which veered between regarding women as available objects, idealizing them (for example, in the courtly love lyric), and despising them—with new, more refined concepts. Honesty and integrity became values in a female aesthetic that encompassed both life and literature. The seventeenth-century "Précieuses" later ridiculed by the playwright Molière, of whom Madeleine de Scudéry was one, considered marriage—in which only the man could choose his partner freely—to be an institution that led to hatred and suffering, and they argued for marriages to have a fixed term, and indeed for free cohabitation. Scudéry herself chose not to marry and also succeeded in freeing herself from her elder brother's guardianship. She saw herself as following in the tradition of the ancient Greek poet Sappho, and held her own successful salon, where her guests could enjoy refined flirting and elevated conversation.

Masterful Men and Womanly Women

ALTERNATIVE WORLDS OF FEELING

"Yes, women are dangerous," declared the German poet Heinrich Heine (1797–1856), who lived as an exile in Paris. He was thinking of women writers, and in particular the French novelist and authority on Germany Madame de Staël. Heine accused her of having a double viewpoint: Women writers, according to him, have "one eye on the paper and the other on a man"; their writing is characterized by "a certain kind of malicious gossip, a cliquishness that they import into literature," while men take up the pen purely for the sake of the subject about which they are writing. By reviling women writers and dismissing them as frivolous, Heine perpetuated the view that creativity is the prerogative of men alone. It was generally held that women existed to embody beauty, not to

create art. And for this reason, Heine considered beautiful women less dangerous than those "who have more intellectual than physical advantages"—a category in which he included Mme de Staël.

In her novel *Corinne* (1807), Mme de Staël argued that genius stood above the sexes. She emphasized that it had female as well as male traits: To have genius was to be capable of great feelings and to have the ability to turn them into art. In Mme de Staël's day, feeling was considered the preserve of women and regarded as something passive. De Staël, by contrast, stressed its active side and spoke of "enthusiasm," which she defined as a love of beauty, an elevation of the spirit, and the enjoyment of a passionate commitment, combined in a state of mind that, however gentle, was also one of strength. She saw this enthusiasm as being infinitely far removed from fanaticism, and in this she knew that she was in accord with the philosopher Immanuel Kant, to whom she devoted a major chapter in her book on Germany, *De l'Allemagne* (1810). The fanatic believes that he or she is in possession of the truth and excludes others from it. By contrast, the enthusiast feels what is attractive and beautiful in all things; this lends an energy that makes him or her capable of great achievement. From these ideas, Mme de Staël constructed a "philosophy of life" before that expression even existed. Only enthusiasm, she wrote, could counteract our tendency to egoism. A goal attained would never bring satisfaction: "We need to perform actions that involve risk; that is what injects enthusiasm into our blood." Delphine and Corinne, the heroines who give their names to the titles of Mme de Staël's novels and who are both idealized portraits of their creator, embody this genuine enthusiasm and readiness to take risks, and consequently become victims of the social conventions of their day. To be enthusiastic and, moreover, to make novels out of such enthusiasm is to take considerable risks, but those risks are what make life interesting and, above all, free. Women who write are not only (at least in men's eyes) dangerous; they also live dangerously, and in the most fortunate cases they do so from choice.

MARY WOLLSTONECRAFT
Painting by John Keenan (*fl.* 1791–1815), *c.* 1793
Private collection

MARY WOLLSTONECRAFT

"That woman is ... degraded by a concurrence of circumstances, is, I think, clear," wrote Mary Wollstonecraft in her *Vindication of the Rights of Woman* in 1792. She compared the position of women with what was often said about the common people: that they must be kept in ignorance, "or the obsequious slaves ... would feel their own consequence and spurn their chains." She continued: "Men ... submit everywhere to oppression ... instead of asserting their birthright, they quietly lick the dust, and say, 'Let us eat and drink, for tomorrow we die.' Women, I argue from analogy, are degraded by the same propensity to enjoy the present moment, and at last despise the freedom which they have not sufficient virtue to struggle to attain."

A year earlier, in 1791, the Frenchwoman Olympe de Gouges had responded to the Declaration of the Rights of Man with a *Déclaration des droits de la femme et de la citoyenne*. She ended up on the scaffold. Wollstonecraft, too, in her defense of the rights of women, was applying and testing the concept of human rights. Her revolutionary treatise anticipated some of the central arguments of the feminist movement. She claimed that women were held in such low esteem on account of their upbringing, which made no attempt to develop their intellectual abilities, but only made them adept at conforming to the role assigned to them. The status of women was linked to that of men—because men's superiority depended on women's subjugation—but the problem was also compounded by women themselves, since, as Wollstonecraft pointed out, far too many women colluded with the men who appeared on the surface to honor them but in fact despised them. Women's lack of independence was partly of their own making: The cult of feminine sensibility reinforced their actual dependence. And so Wollstonecraft called for nothing more nor less than a "revolution in female manners."

This champion of women's rights died at the age of thirty-eight, soon after giving birth to her daughter, the future Mary Shelley, who at age twenty would create that "modern Prometheus" Victor Frankenstein, one of the great mythic figures of the modern age.

GERMAINE DE STAËL

The daughter of a minister in the French government, Anne-Louise-Germaine Necker, baronne de Staël-Holstein, better known as Madame de Staël, was what was called, even before her time, a strong woman: a woman with great self-assurance of manner, who wrote and involved herself in politics. Simone de Beauvoir admired this compatriot of hers, who dominated men with the power of her mind, and in her love affairs had no cause to feel that she was a man's prey. Her lovers, by whom she had a total of five children, included the diplomat Talleyrand; the French minister of war Narbonne; Count Ribbing, the assassin of the Swedish king Gustav III; Souza, the future Portuguese prime minister; and Benjamin Constant, the writer and cofounder of French liberalism.

Mme de Staël was a superb conversationalist, infinitely superior to the German writers whom she visited in their provincial settings. Schiller complained that because of her "quite exceptional readiness of tongue," all he could do was transform himself "completely into a listening ear." Goethe had his own solution: As soon as she announced her imminent arrival, he adopted the strategy of retreat. However, Mme de Staël expressly exempted these princes among German poets from her verdict that there was "nothing more ponderous and fusty, both morally and physically, than German men." Nor did she accuse German women of these failings, even though she found that they generally lacked the "quickness of mind" that makes for lively conversation.

The first edition of Mme de Staël's great study of Germany, *De l'Allemagne*, appeared in 1810. Napoleon intervened personally and had the whole edition—all 10,000 copies of it—pulped. Three years later, the first French edition was published in London, where its author now lived in exile. It sold out immediately, and within a short time around 70,000 copies of the four-volume work had been sold in Europe. This was the book that presented the Germans as the *Volk der Dichter und Denker*—the nation of poets and thinkers—and that shapes to this day the image of Germany among the French.

GERMAINE DE STAËL
Colored lithograph by Henri-Joseph Hesse (1781–1849), after a painting by François Gérard, *c.* 1830

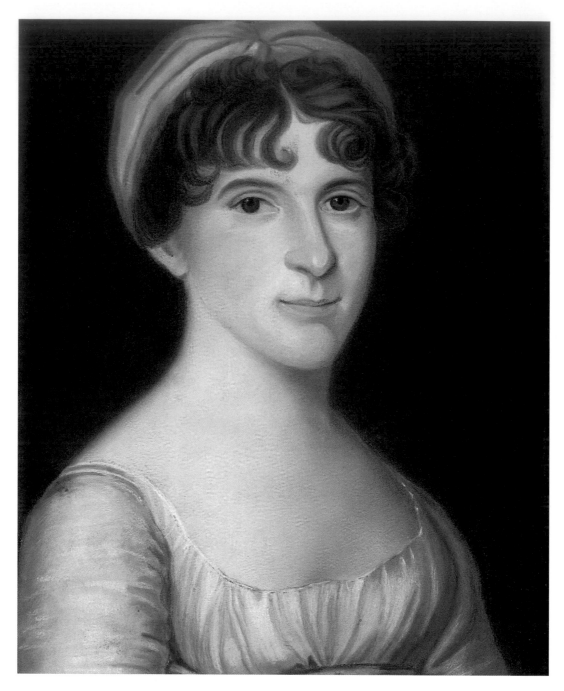

RAHEL VARNHAGEN
Pastel drawing by Peter Friedel (before 1800–before 1814), *c.* 1810
Manuscript Department, Staatsbibliothek zu Berlin – Preussischer
Kulturbesitz

RAHEL VARNHAGEN 1771–1833

At a special soirée in Berlin in spring 1804, a memorable meeting took place between two women writers. Rahel Levin, the German Jewish woman known for her "attic-room gatherings" frequented by aristocrats, the bourgeoisie, and artists, met Mme de Staël, the celebrated author from Paris. The two women talked together at length, and for Levin—who as a writer became known to a wider public only after her death, through the book *Rahel: A Book of Memory for Her Friends*—this conversation provided an opportunity to take Mme de Staël's measure. Eight years earlier, she had professed "love" for her. Now, however, she observed that she found in the Frenchwoman's personality "nothing but a violent wind that I find disagreeable," and that "there is no stillness in her."

There was much that was still and restrained in Rahel Levin, who was an outsider twice over through her Jewish origin and her emancipation as a woman. As a young woman, she used the surname Robert when she traveled, to avoid anti-Jewish prejudice; the few works that she published in her lifetime appeared anonymously. Shortly before her marriage, at the age of forty-three, to the twenty-eight-year-old Karl August Varnhagen von Ense, she was baptized as Friederike Antonie Robert. In Berlin society circles she was condescendingly known as "little Levi," while to her friends and to posterity she remained Rahel.

For Rahel Levin, even more than for Mme de Staël, the cultivation of conversation formed the basis of her writing. This consisted mainly of letters, well over 10,000 of them. They were a substitute for conversation, an extension of the conviviality of the salon. "We Germans," she said, did not yet possess a language that had been "forced through all the pipes of social intercourse" like French—one that was not didactic and artificial like the language of the pulpit but "quite plain and clear and lucid," intelligible to the simplest person. She wanted to find or invent such a language, and with it, herself: "Our language is our life as we live it; I have invented my own life, and so I have not been able to use ready-made expressions as much as many others do. So mine are often clumsy ... but always genuine."

Bettina von Arnim

*B*ettina von Arnim—a granddaughter of Sophie von La Roche, who wrote Germany's first epistolary novel, and sister of the German Romantic writer Clemens Brentano—"came out" as an author in 1835, when she was already fifty years old. Her husband, the writer Achim von Arnim, had died four years earlier, although before his death the couple had increasingly lived apart. Her seven children—Johannes Freimund (it was to him and his mother that the brothers Grimm dedicated their collection of fairy tales), Siegmund, Friedmund, Kühnemund, Maximiliane, Armgart, and Gisela—then ranged in age from twenty-three down to eight.

Von Armin became a writer by looking back to her life as a young single woman; she had not married until she was twenty-six. She edited and published both sides of the correspondence between herself and Goethe and his mother (*Goethe's Correspondence with a Child*, 1835); the writer Karoline von Günderrode (*Die Günderrode*, 1840, dedicated to "the students"); and her brother Brentano (*Clemens Brentano's Garland of Spring Flowers*, published in 1844, two years after Brentano's death). The order in which she published the three bodies of correspondence was the opposite of the order in which the actual exchanges of letters took place.

From the very first book, containing the correspondence with Goethe, childhood is the dominant theme. As von Arnim saw it, the free, unfettered childhood that the poet she idolized had enjoyed was the source of his genius and a mirror-image of her own nature. We see von Arnim, who had come late to writing, canceling out her years of being a wife and mother, and returning to the experiences of her girlhood. It was in those early years that every element of her poetic existence came into being; at that time, as she famously said, her soul was still a passionate dancer who could leap around "to some dance music within myself, which only I can hear and others can't."

BETTINA VON ARNIM
Drawing by Ludwig Emil Grimm (1790–1863), 1810
Goethe-Museum, Frankfurt am Main

George Sand

"Let us be artists," said the twenty-six-year-old Aurore Dupin—by then Mme Dudevant and the mother of two small children—to her friends, and she moved into an attic apartment in Paris. "Here's to the artist's life! Our watchword is freedom!" She took her pen name, Sand, from the student Jules Sandeau, who helped her gain admittance to the world of publishing. Later, when she was using her successive lovers only as her muses, she added the first name George.

Sand's separation from her husband marked the beginning of a meteoric rise from the provinces to the select circles and societies of the French capital, where she fulfilled her ambition of "living by my own means" through her literary activity.

Sand's first novel, which she wrote without Sandeau's assistance and which rapidly brought her fame and a large readership, was *Indiana* (1832). She described the eponymous heroine in these terms: "Indiana is a type: the woman, the weak creature whose function is to portray the repressed passions, or, if you prefer, the passions suppressed by the law; in her we see the will in conflict with necessity, love blindly banging its forehead, until it bleeds, against the obstacles erected by society." Strength of will and a hunger for love that brought her many bloody wounds—that was George Sand. "With machine-like regularity," she wrote for eight hours every day and often into the night as well, sustained by coffee and tobacco, continuing to the point of exhaustion even when she was in pain.

Sand's love affair with the poet Alfred de Musset ended because of her rigid work pattern, which she kept up even during their stay in Venice. While she wrote, Musset consoled himself with alcohol and prostitutes and eventually became very ill (whereupon Sand fell in love with his doctor). Her hunger for love, which she tried to satisfy with lovers who were generally younger than herself, was probably never wholly assuaged. Does this mean that her emancipation was a failure, as some have claimed? The composer Franz Liszt seems to have reached a truer verdict. He wrote to Sand that she was more difficult to console than other people, "For you have never found a loving heart that was feminine enough to love you ..."

JANE AUSTEN

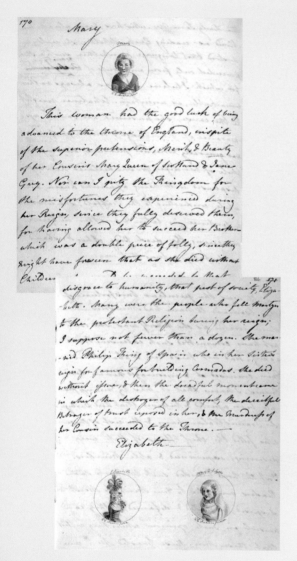

Above: From "The History of England,"
manuscript by Jane Austen, with illustrations
by Cassandra Austen, 1790–93
British Library, London

JANE AUSTEN
Contemporary engraving, after a sketch
by Cassandra Austen (1773–1845)

Emotionalism, it seems, was not to Jane Austen's taste; she preferred strength of character. But this is reflected in her famous characters only where they are in a position to act. Then indeed they pursue their goal, showing resolution and presence of mind, out of genuine conviction, not mere egoism or opportunism. Between choosing their goal and reaching it, however, there is generally an obstacle course of prejudices and conventions to be negotiated, with all the inevitable confusions and failures along the way. To have the right combination of feeling and character is not necessarily to be free; that freedom has to be demonstrated, often not without some suffering.

We know little about Austen's life. "I doubt," wrote her nephew, James Edward Austen-Leigh, "whether it would be possible to mention any other author of note, whose personal obscurity was so complete." We need not see this as the consequence of a woman's modest ambitions. There is good reason to believe that Austen deliberately chose invisibility because she thought it appropriate for a writer. She wanted to be identified with her works, not with the outward features of her life. But our ignorance is also due to a lack of documentary evidence. Austen's sister, Cassandra, to whom we owe the only authentic portrait of the writer (though it is a mere sketch), not only destroyed her own letters to Jane, but also destroyed some of Jane's, or cut sections out of them.

Austen shows us men and women at a time before people's lives came to be shaped by modern ideas of self-realization, with all the demands and consequent stress that these have brought with them. Her main characters, especially the female ones, face whatever life brings bravely, honestly, and without quibbling. They do this out of a sense of what they owe, not to social conventions, but to themselves. Their "nobility of autonomy" derives from a delightful state that the philosopher Jean-Jacques Rousseau called the *sentiment de l'existence*—a state of self-love in which one enjoys nothing but oneself and one's own existence, and is self-sufficient.

ANNE, EMILY, AND CHARLOTTE BRONTË
After a painting by Branwell Brontë (1817–1848)

THE BRONTË SISTERS

*I*n the Brontë family, death appeared with alarming regularity. Maria (b. 1814), the first of six children, contracted tuberculosis at boarding school and died in May 1825 at the age of eleven. Elizabeth (b. 1815) suffered the same fate as her sister; she was just ten. Charlotte (b. 1816), who under the pseudonym of Currer Bell wrote *Jane Eyre, Shirley,* and *Villette,* survived the longest of all the siblings. She lived to the age of thirty-nine, and in the last year of her life married the curate Arthur Bell Nicholls, whose proposal she had earlier rejected because of the need to look after her father. She was pregnant when she died. Branwell (b. 1817), the only son and the great hope of the family, died in 1848, as a failed artist, from the effects of alcoholism. Emily (b. 1818), who as Ellis Bell published six immortal poems as well as the novel *Wuthering Heights,* lived to the age of thirty, while Anne (b. 1820), the least poetic of the three sisters, died in 1849 aged twenty-nine. Anne wrote the novels *Agnes Grey* and *The Tenant of Wildfell Hall,* published under the name Acton Bell. Maria, the Brontës' mother, had died of cancer in 1821. Only their father, Patrick, the curate of Haworth, West Yorkshire, from 1820 onward, lived beyond forty, surviving to the age of eighty-four.

The Brontë children grew up with the fantasy worlds of Angria and Gondal, kingdoms of their own invention nurtured by their intensive reading. A box of wooden soldiers that their father had brought them stimulated their imagination, and they created a vast saga in which historical and invented dukes, captains, despots, and ladies played the chief parts. They devised and performed plays, wrote legends and chronicles, put together magazines, drew maps, and painted pictures. Their life in the lonely parsonage, surrounded by the howling of the wind and the drumming of the rain, was awash with intrigues, battles, and powerful passions, interrupted only by household chores and walks on the lonely moors.

The later writings of the Brontë sisters were in part the product of the intense, obsessive introvertedness of this dream world. Even as adults the Brontës did not cease to be children. Their creative naïveté was combined with relentless

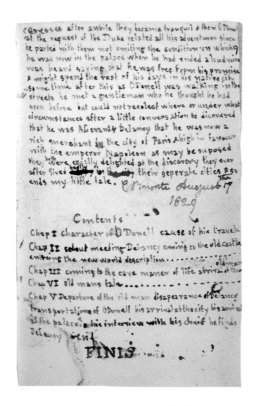

Final page of the manuscript "The Search After Happiness" by Charlotte Brontë, August 17, 1829
British Library, London

earnestness and a total lack of humor and irony; it was under-pinned by a secret contempt for the world of adults and a deep sense of being different and inadequate. The sisters rarely spent time away from the parsonage, or if they did, they returned as soon as possible to their childhood home. The fire in the hearth shed its red, flickering light on the pages of their manuscripts, in which the human psyche is portrayed as a battlefield—full of frightening forebodings of death, full of dread, but also full of fearlessness and impetuosity wreaking terrible havoc.

With the Brontës, feeling is everything. The actions of their heroes and heroines are driven by their hidden and repressed emotions, the gently rippled surface of which conceals seething volcanic forces beneath. In their novels, the three sisters, particularly Emily, studied the inner workings of the heart and found raging madness at its core.

The parsonage at Haworth, West Yorkshire, home of the Brontë sisters

Božena Němcová

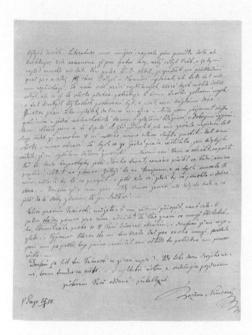

Božena Němcová
Painting by J.V. Hellrich

Above: An original manuscript page
by Němcová

Božena Němcová, the "first modern Czech woman," as she was called, was probably the illegitimate daughter of the sister of the duchess of Sagan. She was adopted by the head groom and grew up in northern Bohemia. At twenty-one she married, and she gave birth to four children in five years. She had spoken only German at home, but her husband introduced her to Czech patriotic circles. Thus it was only relatively late that Němcová—who became a national legend after her death—began to read Czech books and learn Czech grammar and spelling.

The beautiful Němcová became a writer under the influence of the young poet Václav Bolemír Nebeský. Nebeský was not her only lover, as she confessed in a surprisingly candid letter to her husband. Yet she was left with nothing but disappointment and resentment: "In vain I looked for a love like the love I felt myself. I wanted a man whom I could have revered ... but I found in men only crude tyrants, only lords and masters ... My heart has become filled with bitterness and defiance. You men possessed my body and my actions, all that I am outwardly, but my longings roamed far away." She concludes, "I wanted to fill that emptiness in my heart, but I did not know what with." When she was at her lowest ebb, groping her way blindly like a pilgrim in the dark, a new star of love rose for her. As she wrote to a friend: "It lighted the way for me, and I followed it." That star was literature. As soon as Němcová started writing, she felt that she was in a different world.

Some aspects of that world are portrayed too idyllically for our modern tastes. But Němcová's most famous book, *The Grandmother* (1855), is more than just a fairy tale recounted for her own consolation. Where life brings adversity, Němcová shows the resilience and endurance with which children and the archetypal grandmother figure are able to withstand it. Through Němcová, simple people make their entry into both Czech and world literature, unobtrusively resisting with all their meager strength as the thunderous roar of history sweeps over them.

HARRIET BEECHER STOWE
Undated photograph

HARRIET BEECHER STOWE

"So this is the little lady who made this big war," Abraham Lincoln is supposed to have said in 1862 of the author of *Uncle Tom's Cabin; or, Life Among the Lowly*. This is certainly an overstatement of the sociopolitical impact of Harriet Beecher Stowe's most famous book. The novel was not the cause of the American Civil War, but Stowe did portray her times through feelings, which she formed into effective scenes. She wanted to write in the same way that a painter paints: "My vocation is simply that of a painter. ... There is no arguing with *pictures*, and everybody is impressed with them, whether they mean to be or not."

One of the most moving images, in which cruelty, goodness, and indignation are brought vividly to life, occurs in the scene in which Uncle Tom dies after being viciously beaten by the henchmen of the slave-owner Legree. Just before he takes his last breath, he is found at last, after months of fruitless searching, by the young and kindhearted George. He greets him with a cry from the soul: "O, Mas'r George! What a thing 'tis to be a Christian!" Yet it is not goodness but anger that has the last word in this scene: "George turned, and, with one indignant blow, knocked Legree flat upon his face; and, as he stood over him, blazing with wrath and defiance, he would have formed no bad personification of his great namesake triumphing over the dragon."

Even contemporaries noted that the author's handling of this death scene was very much in the tradition of the sentimental women's novel. Uncle Tom, goodness personified, has every quality that a woman was expected to have, and reacts as a woman would be expected to react. The scene thus blends together the position of slaves and that of women. In the slave, Tom, it was possible to discern a woman's soul, with which female readers could identify. After all, they themselves were victims of a society dominated by men, as Mary Wollstonecraft had pointed out decades earlier. But they could not, any more than the black slaves, hope for a dragon-slayer to lead them out of subjugation.

From Pure of Heart to Fiery Rebellion
THE DISCOVERY OF CHILDHOOD

In 1900, right at the turn of the century, the Swedish educationalist Ellen Key published a book that very quickly achieved huge sales and was translated into many languages. Its title, *The Century of the Child*, was both a prediction and a program. The author called for a radical re-evaluation of the child. Instead of regarding the child merely as a preliminary stage in the formation of the adult and constantly interfering in its development, she argued, people should treat the child as a separate entity that could be understood only on its own terms. Those who were children at that time would be growing up in the new century, and it was hoped that they would be happier than preceding generations.

Ever since the eighteenth century, a gradual change had been taking place in which the extended family household was being replaced by the nuclear family, consisting only of parents and their children. Now the family was supported no longer by the communal labor of all its members, including the women and children and also the servants, but instead by the husband's employment outside the family. Freed from the need to work from an early age, children could concentrate on learning for life and learning how to live. A growing body of literature written for children and young people taught appropriate behavior and moral values, and schooled their intellect and imagination. It introduced children to the challenges of the wider world, for example, through adventure stories. In due course, there were books for adolescents that no longer wagged an admonishing

Selma Lagerlöf

finger at them but increasingly responded to their needs and recognized the legitimacy of their world. These books dealt with the confusions and tensions that derive from the gulf between young people's notions of life and the real, adult world. Sometimes this conflict brings disaster and even death to the young protagonist, but sometimes he or she is able to resolve his or her problems and move on, leaving childhood behind. Very often the adult world is made the butt of mockery. This has its attraction for adults, too—or even especially for them—since they are also victims of the reality principle.

Women traditionally remained more in touch with the world of childhood than did men, who faced the necessity—or enjoyed the privilege—of going out into a hostile world and returning home with money in their pockets. The woman's role was that of mediating between the child's world and the adult world, between wishful thinking and reason, fantasy and reality. This inevitably shaped the way in which women writers for children and adolescents regarded themselves and their work. From Johanna Spyri and Astrid Lindgren to J.K. Rowling, these women writers show the world in a kind of limbo where two perspectives intersect: that of the child, who feels impelled to oppose the grown-ups and yet wants to become a grown-up himself or herself; and that of the adult, who is involved in the upbringing and education of children and yet still has a small child somewhere deep inside.

Johanna Spyri

JOHANNA SPYRI

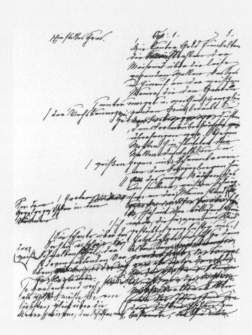

JOHANNA SPYRI
Undated photograph with signature

Above: "A Quiet House," unpublished manuscript from Spyri's papers, undated

The cast of characters in Johanna Spyri's world-famous children's story, which has been translated into fifty languages, is not exactly promising: a homeless orphan; her misanthropic grandfather, embittered by the death of his wife and son and living as a recluse in the mountains, shunning social contact; a monosyllabic boy with learning difficulties who lives in great poverty and has to work during the summer vacation; a girl whose depression has led to physical paralysis; her father, who, instead of taking care of her, is constantly away traveling; and a governess whose sinister educational methods cause psychological harm to the children in her charge.

We are talking about the story of Heidi. The full title of the first volume—*Heidi's Years of Learning and Travel*—is unmistakably modeled on the titles of Goethe's two novels tracing the development of the young Wilhelm Meister. Spyri added a subtitle that welcomed adult readers, too, calling it "A story for children and for those who love children."

All the characters are ultimately healed and restored as they cast off the constricting norms of bourgeois convention and follow a simpler, more natural way of life. Spyri's Heidi is like a sister of Rousseau's Émile—a version of Eve before the Fall, an unspoiled child with healing powers, in whose pure heart the spirit of the divine is still alive.

Spyri's father was a doctor and, as he treated his patients in the family home, she became familiar with mental illness from a very early age. Her mother was a devout Pietist who wrote religious poetry. Johanna married, moved with her husband to Zurich, became pregnant—and fell into a severe depression. She felt imprisoned and had a sense of being wholly controlled by other people. The fact that she found no joy in being a mother burdened her with a sense of guilt. It was not until twenty years later—when she was forty-four, and her only son (who was to die at the age of twenty-nine) had just completed his grammar-school education—that she found true fulfillment. She began to write and within a very few years had become a successful author.

"After breakfast, taking Mr. Benjamin Bunny to pasture at the edge of the cabbage bed with his leather dog-lead, I heard a rustling, and out came a little wild rabbit to talk to him ... The little animal, evidently a female, and of shabby appearance ... advanced ..., its face twitching with excitement and admiration for the beautiful Benjamin, who at length caught sight of it round a cabbage, and immediately bolted. He probably took it for Miss Hutton's cat."

The journal that Beatrix Potter kept from the age of sixteen in her own code writing is full of such humorous observations. This particular entry is dated August 20, 1892—when Potter was twenty-six—and it would be another ten years before *The Tale of Peter Rabbit* appeared, first brought out privately but soon afterward reissued, with color illustrations, by a commercial publisher. The tone of the story, however, and its central figure—a little rabbit making his escape through a garden—is already there in the diary. With its blend of realistic observation and fable, together with its finely detailed illustrations and an unusually small format, *Peter Rabbit* has become a classic of English children's literature.

Potter had a sheltered but lonely childhood. Her parents did not send her to school or allow her to have playmates. She spent her time in the family's large house or in the garden, keeping a menagerie of rabbits, hedgehogs, and mice, drawing the animals outside her window and the plants in the flower beds, copying museum exhibits, and studying natural history. She was thirty-nine before she got engaged, and her fiancé died the same year.

Potter's anthropomorphic approach to nature takes on greater significance and seriousness when we see it as her rejection of a very different tendency that was epitomized by the practice of vivisection, the dissection of live animals for research purposes. "Vivisection is a crime perpetrated wholly and entirely by men," wrote a German woman contemporary of Potter's, arguing that women had a duty to combat this evil practice.

BEATRIX POTTER
Photograph showing the author at the door of her farmhouse, Hill Top, at Sawrey in the English Lake District, 1907

SELMA LAGERLÖF

Above: Front cover of the first postwar German edition of *The Wonderful Adventures of Nils*, 1948

Twice the Tom-Thumblike Nils Holgersson unselfishly forgoes the chance to return to life among fully grown people: the first time so as to help a despairing student, the second to save the life of the gander Martin—on whose back Nils flies around Sweden—when his owners plan to wring his neck. Nils's mother has shut the gander into the henhouse and intends to roast him for the table. Nils rushes to his aid and in so doing involuntarily lets his parents see him in his diminutive form. At that moment, he returns to normal size, loses his understanding of the language of animals, and ceases to be a child. When children admit to their parents that they are little creatures who are dependent on them, they have achieved the degree of maturity needed to leave their childish status behind.

The Wonderful Adventures of Nils (1906) is an adventure story, a novel tracing an individual's development, a fairy tale, and a factual book all rolled into one. It all began when Selma Lagerlöf, a teacher, was commissioned by the Swedish Ministry of Education to write a geography textbook about Sweden for use in primary schools. The influence of Rudyard Kipling's *Jungle Book* (1894) is unmistakable: Just as Mowgli lives among the wolves, so Nils lives with the wild geese. Nils's fairy-tale reduction to a miniature figure allows the author to alternate constantly between a bird's-eye and a worm's-eye view. In this way, the reader gets both an overall perspective (Sweden from above) and a close-up of details that would otherwise go unnoticed. A hip problem restricted Lagerlöf to the position of an observer in real life, but here, in fiction, she achieved mobility.

In 1909, Lagerlöf became the first woman to receive the Nobel Prize for Literature. It has since been awarded to nine more women: Grazia Deledda (1926), Sigrid Undset (1928), Pearl Buck (1938), Gabriela Mistral (1945), Nelly Sachs (1966), Nadine Gordimer (1991), Toni Morrison (1993), Wislawa Szymborska (1996), and Elfriede Jelinek (2004). Lagerlöf's blend of rationality and mysticism is characteristic of many writers of that time, both male and female, who responded to the *fin-de-siècle* mood of uncertainty by seeking new modes of expression and striving for the improvement of life in general.

ASTRID LINDGREN

strid Lindgren let it be known that the name Pippi Longstocking was invented by her daughter, who once, when seriously ill, asked for a story: "Tell me about Pippi Longstocking."

Lindgren's daughter made a good choice. "Pippi" in Swedish means madness. And "Longstocking" accidentally echoes the English term "bluestocking," which was often used to describe educated women, some of whom were even writers. "Let not women write poetry:/ They should try to be poems themselves," advised the clumsily worded poem *Bluestockings* (1887) by Oscar Blumenthal. The word itself dates back to the eighteenth century, when a certain gentleman who could not afford the black silk stockings that went with evening dress was allowed by Lady Montagu to attend her London salon wearing stockings of blue cotton. From that time on, guests at such literary and aesthetic gatherings presided over by women were known as "bluestockings."

One of Lindgren's models was the girls' story *Anne of Green Gables* (1908), by the Canadian writer L.M. Montgomery. It is the tale of an elderly brother and sister who decide to adopt an orphaned boy, but are sent a little girl instead: eleven-year-old Anne Shirley, with her red hair and freckles, who talks non-stop, is never short of ideas, and possesses daring, intelligence, and a fiery temperament. In Anne, Montgomery created a new type of girl; in Pippi Longstocking, theatrical and rebellious traits are added.

Pippi Longstocking was created in 1941. In 1944, Lindgren put the first Pippi stories down on paper. The manuscript was rejected by the publishers Bonniers (the author jokingly signed off her covering letter "Hoping that you won't alert the child welfare officer"), but in 1945 it won Lindgren first prize in a competition, and the stories were then published. The book and its heroine were controversial. Educationalists, and other people, too, detected in them an attack on authority and a demand that children be given more freedom—and they were absolutely right.

ASTRID LINDGREN
Photograph by Bo Johansson, 1991

Writing to Live and Living to Write
ECCENTRIC ORBITS

Eccentrics are defined as characters who are strikingly different from the social norms, people who do not act in a conventional manner but tend toward exaggerated behavior and taste. Someone who merely behaves a little differently from others is by no means an eccentric. We are more likely to call such a person an outsider. To be an eccentric, the person has to be aware of being an outsider and be completely open about it. Far from concealing his or her status as an outsider, the eccentric makes something of it, shaping it into what he or she finds a congenial way of life. Divergent behavior plus self-stylization—these are what make an eccentric personality.

Until well into the twentieth century, women were outsiders in the world of writing. But they became increasingly happy to be in that situation. They consciously cultivated ways of diverging from normal behavior and sought out roles in which they could be simultaneously actors and spectators. As we can see from the personality and the work of Anna Akhmatova, it is perfectly possible to combine self-stylization with writing poetry that speaks with the utmost integrity about life. The very choice of her pen name—her original surname was Gorenko—was part of the shaping of her legend. Joseph Brodsky, who knew her personally, commented: "The five 'a's' in 'Anna Akhmatova' had a hypnotic effect, and placed the bearer of that name at the very head of the alphabet of Russian poetry. You could say it was her first successful line." Another characteristic element in the self-stylization of a woman poet is to convey an impression of helplessness in the face of the mundane realities of life. Ingeborg Bachmann achieved this to perfection.

An eccentric way of life does not have to be limited to an unusual identity. After Karen Blixen's African adventure ended in disaster, she discovered that the greatest trap in life is one's own identity, whether self-chosen or imposed by others. "I will not be one person again ... I will be always many persons from now," a character says in her story "The Dreamers." Literature is a game of identities, perhaps especially sexual identity. Here Virginia Woolf went farther than most others, notably with the figure of Orlando, in her novel of that name. Orlando's sex undergoes a change as the story progresses and the centuries pass. He, or she, finally matures into an independent woman writer of the twentieth century who combines both male and female characteristics within herself. Here literature and the life of a writer take up an eccentric position in relation to the accepted boundaries of sexual identity, playing with them instead of slavishly conforming to them.

SIDONIE GABRIELLE COLETTE

"*She* is the only really great woman writer in France, a really great writer," enthused Simone de Beauvoir, describing Colette in a letter to her American lover, Nelson Algren, in 1948, and she continued, in her slightly quaint English: "She was once the most beautiful woman. She danced in music halls, slept with a lot of men, wrote pornographic novels and then good novels. She loved country, flowers, beasts, and making love, and then she loved too the most sophisticated life; she slept with women, too. She was fond of food and wine—well, she loved all good living things, and she spoke beautifully about them. Now she is seventy-five years old and has still the most fascinating eyes and a nice triangular cat face." Meeting Colette—who was thirty-five years older than herself—meant a great deal to de Beauvoir, for, as she confessed to Algren, "I was in love with her, through her books, when I was a girl."

Sidonie Gabrielle Colette grew up in a small village in Burgundy. At twenty she married Henry Gauthier-Villars, the son of her father's publisher. Gauthier-Villars was fourteen years her senior and wrote under the name of Willy. The couple took a flat in Paris. When she separated from her husband at the age of thirty-three, Mme Willy was determined to earn her own living. She made ends meet by working not only as a writer and journalist but also as an actress, dancer, and nude artiste in variety shows, with all the inevitable accompanying scandals. Colette was as familiar with the *demi-monde* of music halls and the lesbian salon of the American writer Natalie Barney as she was with the "official" cultural scene. She saw herself as a "vagabond" (the title she gave to the autobiographical novel she published in 1911), a drifter, a rootless wanderer. And yet Colette's mother did not worry too much about her daughter, believing that she was right not to stake everything on love. Whatever Colette did, she did with a kind of innocent pride and unwavering professionalism, without ever being wholly absorbed by it.

As a young girl, there was a period when Colette persuaded her mother to wake her at half past three each morning. Then, in the blue Burgundian morning light, she would run alone

COLETTE
Undated photograph

Above: Undated postcard advertising Colette's "Claudine" novels

COLETTE
Painting by Emilie Charmy (1877–1974), 1921
Private collection

down to the nearby river, then make a big arc through the woods, "like a dog looking for a kill," and drink water from two hidden springs. "In that way, and at that hour, I grew conscious of my own worth," she claimed, much like the young George Sand, who roamed the fields with a gun instead of going to the debutantes' ball. And Colette can indeed seem like a modern version of Sand, except that the nineteenth-century mask of virtue is shed in favor of total dedication to what Colette called the "inexorable force," the combination of impulses that we call sensuality. The title of Judith Thurman's biography of Colette, *Secrets of the Flesh*, is an apt one.

Two themes are especially characteristic of Colette's novels: the growing-up and sexual awakening of a young woman, and the love of a self-confident, mature woman for a younger man. But Colette also described, again and again, the harmonious, easy relationships between women: their conversations about the right lipstick and the most becoming hairstyle, about day-to-day worries and the ups and downs of love—the spontaneous, warm-hearted intimacy between women that is often so much less burdensome than relationships with the opposite sex. That Colette and her work were never taken very seriously—a fact that did not worry her—may be due to her love of trivial things and her refusal to take a tragic view of life. "Happiness lies in living like everyone else but being like no one else," Simone de Beauvoir said. By that measure, Colette had a happy life.

1902.

MILES FRANKLIN

*M*iles Franklin was an Australian girl prodigy, but her early fame did not usher in the glittering career that the critics had foretold for her. The English publisher of her autobiographical novel *My Brilliant Career*, written when she was only sixteen and published in 1901, removed the question mark she had placed after the adjective, but in fact it was prophetic. For decades, Franklin published nothing that could stand comparison with that first book, which, despite its unevenness and outmoded style, would always remain her most famous work.

My Brilliant Career is the story of a young girl finding her identity. Receiving a proposal of marriage from a young and virtuous landowner, she at first rejects him in no uncertain terms but later accepts him when he loses his fortune and sets out to make his own way in the world, only to retract her promise, despite her own extremely pitiable situation, when he returns, mature and immensely rich. The contradictory personality of the female protagonist, Sybilla Penelope, contains many elements of the author herself: Unladylike and prickly, but also honest, thoughtful, and longing for love, she is still a figure with whom girls on the verge of womanhood, in particular, can readily identify.

In 1906, Franklin emigrated to Chicago, where she worked for the Women's Trade Union League. Nine years later, she moved to London, where she earned her living as a hospital cook and journalist. She continued to live an unsettled life until 1932, when, at the age of fifty-three, she finally returned to Australia. By this time she had built up a career—not quite so glittering, because she concealed her identity—as a writer of family chronicles. She wrote them as Brent of Bin Bin, a name that evoked early Australian settlers and cattle-breeders. Only after Franklin's death did it emerge that the writer behind the pseudonym was in fact the author of *My Brilliant Career*, although her continuing popularity resulting from that first novel had enabled her to promote the works of "Brent of Bin Bin" very effectively.

Miles Franklin
Photograph, 1902
State Library of New South Wales, Sydney

Virginia Woolf

Above: Front cover of *Jacob's Room*,
first published in 1922

Virginia Woolf
Photograph by George Charles Beresford
(1864–1938), 1902

irginia Woolf's life was a series of waves: a Victorian childhood; the liberated atmosphere of the Bloomsbury Group of writers, artists, and intellectuals; success and recognition as an author; then suicide at the age of fifty-nine. Beyond that, Woolf's name stands for the unusual combination of an avant-garde writer who gave a voice to the inner life of human beings, and a publisher who, together with her husband, Leonard, produced the works of the literary avant garde. Her novel *Jacob's Room* appeared in the same year, 1922, as James Joyce's *Ulysses* and T.S. Eliot's *The Waste Land*, and represented her literary breakthrough. It was published by the Woolfs' own Hogarth Press, where, to begin with, Virginia worked as editor and typesetter while her husband was the printer and business manager. The Hogarth Press gave Virginia independence as a writer. She was able to describe herself as the only woman of her day in England who was "free to write what I like."

Woolf was such an outstanding writer not because of but despite her mental illness. The experience of writing must have been an ambivalent one for her. She lived in constant fear that people might see no sense in her work, that they might think her mad rather than brilliant.

Yet Woolf was a shrewd, incorruptible, and tireless observer of life and of her times. As an author, she let the borderline experiences that characterized her bouts of illness enter her literary work, too, giving us invaluable insights into the fragile and precarious nature of human existence. Nothing was more important to Woolf than the wholeness of her perception and the integrity of her art. Her life, marked by illness, fear, and suffering, was not one of oppression. It was the life of a heroic woman who could write to her husband, before leaving him forever: "I don't think two people could have been happier than we have been."

KAREN BLIXEN

KAREN BLIXEN
Photograph, 1923

Above: *Masai. Moran and Ndito*, one of Blixen's
final drawings, 1960

Anything would be preferable to being a writer. So said the young Karen Christentze Dinesen, whose father was of the landed gentry and whose mother came from a family of prominent Copenhagen merchants. She listed the things she preferred: "travel, dancing, life, the freedom to paint pictures." At this time, under the pen name of Osceola, she had already published several novellas, one of which contains the sentence, "Everyone has the right to choose his own destiny, regardless of laws established by others ..." Karen's marriage in 1914 to her cousin, Baron Bror Blixen-Finecke, gave her the opportunity to escape from the "infinitely dreary existence" of a rich young girl to the darkly alluring world of the Kikuyu, Masai, and Somalis of the then British East Africa Protectorate.

Eighteen years later, Blixen's African adventure ended with the compulsory sale of her coffee plantation and the liquidation of the Karen Coffee Co. Ltd, which she ran. It was failure on all fronts: Both her marriage and her love affair with the English aristocrat Denys Finch Hatton had also come to an end. At forty-seven, she was once again financially dependent on her family, from whom she had never really escaped.

The philosopher Hannah Arendt saw this time as the decisive, indispensable turning point in Blixen's life: "Only when she had lost what had been her life, her home in Africa and her lover, only when she returned to Rungstedlund as a complete 'failure,' with nothing but sorrow, anxieties, and memories, did she become an artist and achieve the 'success' that she would never otherwise have achieved." The stories Blixen now wrote, and the memoir *Out of Africa* (1937), which transfigured the reality of her experiences (this was the book, published under the name of Isak Dinesen, that made her world-famous), show what Thomas Mann called the "perspective by which art turns life into myth." Blixen's life followed the pattern of "dying in order to become something new," and was a rich source of inspiration for her writings.

ELSE LASKER-SCHÜLER

ELSE LASKER-SCHÜLER
Bridal photograph, 1894

Above: Manuscript of the poem "Saul,"
from *Hebrew Ballads* (1913)

"I have never worked out a system, as clever women do, never fixed a philosophy in place anywhere, as even cleverer men do, I have not built myself an Ark. I am not bound, there are words of mine lying around everywhere ... I have always been the Prince of Thebes," wrote the poet Else Lasker-Schüler. Prince Yussuf of Thebes, ruler of the new kingdom of art, was one of the many fantasy personages into whose skin she would slip. She wanted to put reality into fancy dress, giving herself and her lovers and friends new, fantastical names so that, as she wrote, "we can play ... playing is everything." Lasker-Schüler led an eccentric, consciously antibourgeois life in the bohemian world of Berlin and held court in the Romanisches Café as an Oriental fairy-tale princess, receiving the homage of the leading lights of Expressionism (of whom she herself was one). Her poems and also her prose have a strong element of dialogue: Many of her poems are not only dedicated to friends but also actually address them by their fairy-tale names. There were some who suspected that beneath Lasker-Schüler's capricious insouciance and mystical dreaming there lurked a sense of emptiness. "I am the last nuance of desolation, nothing further is possible," she wrote at age forty-three, after separating from her second husband, Herwarth Walden, editor of the periodical *Der Sturm*.

If the career of this "artist of life" took an unconventional course, this was not only because she traveled through Expressionist terrain and was always searching for forgotten, higher realities. In May 1933, her books were thrown on to the Nazi bonfires, and Lasker-Schüler, who was Jewish, fled to Switzerland. From there, she made several trips to Jerusalem, and in 1939 the outbreak of war prevented her from returning to Zurich. In Jerusalem, she published her last collection of poems, *My Blue Piano*, a farewell to "forgotten golden legends," written "with a late, sunken heart," as she says in her afterword: "1000 and 2 years old, I have outgrown fairy tales."

Milena Jesenská

"*S*he is a living fire such as I have never seen," wrote Franz Kafka of Milena Jesenská, who is now known to us chiefly as the recipient of his *Letters to Milena*; her letters to him are lost. Their meeting came about because Jesenská wanted to translate Kafka into Czech. This young woman from Prague, whose adolescent years had involved some wild escapades, was at that time living in Vienna with her first husband, Ernst Pollak, an author with writer's block, and was associating with the literary habitués of the Café Central and later of the Café Herrenhof. She earned her living by occasional commissions, and was looking for ways to get her work published.

Although Jesenská moved in literary circles, she did not regard herself as a literary writer but as a journalist, which at that time was viewed as a lesser occupation. She worked as a correspondent and writer of articles on culture and society for periodicals and weekly journals. Even in her earliest articles, the typical "Milena tone" is recognizable: unpretentious and unromantic, casual and spontaneous. But above all, Jesenská looks and listens closely, and she is convinced of the importance of communicating fully with the reader. She herself said that the style of her articles was derived from that of letter-writing, thus placing herself in the long tradition of women whose distinctive way of writing developed from the habit of correspondence. She once remarked that the only thing she could really write was love letters, and "ultimately, that is what all my articles are."

In the mid-1930s, Jesenská, whose cultural articles had focused particularly on aspects of "modern times" and who had drawn closer to the left-wing avant garde, switched to political reporting. Her biographer, Alena Wagnerová, has called her political articles, which were well researched and politically committed, *Love Letters to Central Europe*. In 1940, because of her work for a banned journal, Jesenská was deported to Ravensbrück concentration camp, where she died four years later.

MILENA JESENSKÁ
Passport photograph with signature, c. 1916

ANNA AKHMATOVA

Anna Akhmatova—as Anna Andreyevna Gorenko called herself, after a Tartar grandmother—hated to be called a "poetess." She was the star of the Acmeists, a group active before the First World War who wanted to bring back comprehensibility to Russian poetry. They no longer took their inspiration from music, like the Symbolists, but favored architecture and painting. The Russian-Jewish painter and book designer Natan Altman painted a portrait of Akhmatova, introducing Cubist elements; the artist Amedeo Modigliani also produced a cycle of drawings of the young, newly married poet while she was visiting Paris. They had probably struck up a friendship as a result of their shared admiration of the poetry of Paul Verlaine.

In the years following 1910, there was a real Akhmatova cult in St. Petersburg. Her devotees saw her as the embodiment of the modern young woman, and even imitated her gestures, voice, and dress. However, in post-Revolutionary Russia, Akhmatova became more and more of an outsider, and in 1946, Stalin's cultural commissar, Andrei Zhdanov, was still denouncing her work as the "poetry of a socialite gone wild, who trots back and forth between boudoir and prayer stool." Besides her strength and toughness, Akhmatova's contemporaries always stressed her homelessness. Constantly having to stay with friends, the poet possessed few books (she knew by heart the most important ones, including Dante, Pushkin, Dostoevsky, Eliot, and the epic of Gilgamesh) and carried around with her only a small case with her manuscripts. She had adapted to surviving in the most adverse conditions, which included a ban on publishing her work that lasted for decades. Having thus renounced "all earthly gain," Akhmatova ultimately saw herself as merely a "guest" in life, and regarded living as a "habit." But one thing—her love of beauty—remained, and she referred to it in the poem "Last Rose," written in her final years:

Above: Manuscript of a poem
by Akhmatova, 1910

ANNA AKHMATOVA
Painting by N.I. Altman (1889–1970), 1914

Lord! You see I am tired
Of living and dying and resurrection.
Take everything, but grant that I may feel
That freshness of this crimson rose again.

AGATHA CHRISTIE

gatha Christie was not an eccentric—unlike the murderers in her sixty-six detective novels. Although they may dispatch their victims in a tidy and civilized way, they nonetheless embody that dangerous outer edge of society where alienation and abnormality tip over into madness. Christie never analyzed her murderers' motives sociologically; her explanation for a criminal nature was insanity, which she attributed to a genetic flaw: "A malformation of the grey cells may coincide quite easily with the face of a Madonna."

Christie was one of those daughters of the English upper classes who grew up in the care of a nanny and had little conventional education. Instead, she gleaned her knowledge from the wonderland of her parents' library. It was in her childhood, too, that she developed her love of secrets. When, as a five-year-old, she discovered that her governess repeated things she had confided, she vowed to keep everything to herself in future.

Convinced of her talent, her widowed mother encouraged Christie, while still in her teens, to write novels and stories, and writing became a habit she enjoyed. As she observed, with a touch of self-irony, it took the place of embroidering cushions or painting china. All the same, she rapidly achieved the success that made her the most widely read woman writer in the world and that owed much to her—very discreet—professionalism.

The period between the two world wars was the golden age of crime fiction, the secret of which, according to W.H. Auden, is "to conceal [the murderer's] demonic pride from the other characters and from the reader." In Christie, this concealment was taken to such lengths that in *The Murder of Roger Ackroyd* (1926), her most perfect, though also most controversial, whodunit, it is the narrator himself who is finally unmasked as the murderer. Christie's fellow crime writer Dorothy L. Sayers admiringly acknowledged that she, like everyone else, had been successfully hoodwinked.

AGATHA CHRISTIE
Photograph, 1962

ERIKA MANN
Photograph, *c.* 1930

ERIKA MANN

1905–1969

*I*f we are to believe her father, Thomas Mann, who created a portrait of his eldest child in his story "Disorder and Early Sorrow," the young Erika Mann was capable of "claiming, in a high, quavering, vulgarly twittering voice, that she is a shopgirl who has an illegitimate child, a son with sadistic tendencies who, when he was out in the country recently, tormented a cow in such an unspeakable way that no Christian could bear to watch." And Mann did start off as an actress, going on tour with her brother Klaus's early plays. The director was the actor Gustaf Gründgens, to whom she was briefly married. Later Mann married another homosexual artist, the poet W.H. Auden, but only in order to acquire British citizenship. She too was drawn chiefly to her own sex.

In 1928, Mann began to write, producing cultural articles and commentaries for the press. The following year saw the publication of *All the Way Round*, a book that she and Klaus wrote jointly about their trip around the world. Subsequent publications included children's books and material for the topical cabaret "The Pepper Mill," which opened in Munich in January 1933 and continued from March of that year in Zurich.

Recognizing what seemed to be the most promising role for herself at the time, Mann noted in 1931 that there was a new kind of writer about: "the woman who writes reportage, whether in essays, plays, or novels. It is not confessional, she is not pouring out her heart, her own fate is left quietly to one side, the woman is reporting instead of confessing." Mann was in the same position as many other people during that period. The Nazi seizure of power was forcing them to think seriously about politics in a way that they had not done before.

Following the family's emigration to the United States, Mann undertook lecture tours there, reporting on Germany, working as a war correspondent, and finally acting as an observer at the Nuremberg Trials. Shortly after the end of the war and Klaus's subsequent suicide, she embarked on writing about her father's life and work, a task that continued long after his death in 1955.

Ingeborg Bachmann

With the benefit of hindsight, we may recognize links between writers whose affinity was not so obvious to their contemporaries. The Austrian Ingeborg Bachmann counted Sylvia Plath (see pages 104–105) among the writers "who have experienced hell," and who will be considered among the first because they were among the last. This applies equally to herself. Many things may separate Bachmann and Plath—their mother tongue, their country—but they share essential features, not least their view of themselves as writers.

In considering Bachmann and Plath, it is difficult to avoid the word "martyr." Art was their religion, and the absolute nature of its demands made them subject to inescapable suffering. According to this creed, it is neither joy nor pleasure, neither sorrow nor faith, but only fear, pain, and suffering that qualify us to be the elect, if we aspire to be poets.

Plath noted in her journal that writing is "a religious act" and the heaviest responsibility in the world. One might also say that to write is to take up the cross as an exemplary sufferer for the sake of a possible resurrection in poetry. When Plath says in her poem "Lady Lazarus" (1962) that dying is "an art, like everything else," and that she does it "exceptionally well," she is not just anticipating her suicide a few months later, but also making a statement about writing: It is an act of self-obliteration, since that is the only way to experience a different state of being.

"But I lie alone/ Hemmed in by ice and covered in wounds," Bachmann wrote in her *Songs in Flight*, expressing the longing of a suffering human being to be released from the deathly cold of the world: "Set me free! I cannot go on dying!" Earlier, in her poem "Exile," she had described the poet as a dead person who can no longer live among human beings. The same idea is expressed by Plath: Writing is the most exquisite of all the different "ways of dying," because poetry is a fire that not only burns us but also brings us face to face with the divine.

INGEBORG BACHMANN
Undated photograph

SYLVIA PLATH

*L*ike Ingeborg Bachmann, Sylvia Plath is much revered. In each case, a spectacular death—Plath's suicide at the age of thirty, Bachmann's fatal injuries resulting from an accidental fire after she had taken alcohol and pills—laid the foundation for the elevation to mythical status of a woman who had exhausted herself in the service of poetry. In both cases, there was ample evidence that behind the poetic drama of the writer there also lay the inner, psychological drama of a failed attempt at emancipation.

Each began her career as a poet by deliberately adopting a certain persona. Plath liked to present herself as the radiant all-American girl, a winner of bursaries and prizes, who gave all her suitors the brush-off and finally married the poet Ted Hughes, whom fate had destined for her as her equal. The image, however, concealed an extreme degree of perfectionism and a compulsion to achieve. In the end, Plath's recurrent depression proved too much for her.

What struck contemporaries about Bachmann was her uncompromising nature. Her editor at the Piper publishing house said that she saw writing as a trial of strength. "She had set her heart on being able to do whatever she wanted. And in fact she did achieve everything she wanted," said someone who did not much like her. But even Bachmann became dependent on alcohol and medicinal drugs—if not before, then certainly after the breakup of her affair with the playwright and novelist Max Frisch, which she felt to be a betrayal of love. She interpreted her addictions and fits of despair as signs that she had been "defeated by reality" and as a reaction to a hurt that could not be assuaged. No one, she said, was driven mad by writing; they only went mad "in the same way as anyone who doesn't write … through the loss of their self-respect, the threat to their existence." In her essay on Plath, which she entitled "Tremendum"—an allusion to the religious experience of dread in the presence of the divine—Bachmann wrote, "Illness is sheer horror, it is a thing whose outcome is death."

SYLVIA PLATH
Photograph by Rollie McKenna
(1918–2003), 1959
National Portrait Gallery, Smithsonian
Institution, Washington, D.C.

ELSA MORANTE

The Italian writer Elsa Morante's four novels span a whole century. *House of Liars* (1948) takes us back to the period around 1900, and shows us a woman who chooses enchantment in preference to reality. *Arturo's Island* (1957), set in the 1920s and 1930s, is an account of a painful farewell to a paradisiacal childhood and youth. *History* (1974) counts the cost of the Second World War and depicts the everyday life of innocent women, children, and animals who are helplessly exposed to the forces of history. And *Aracoeli* (1982), set in the postwar period, describes a son's attempts to discover the secret of his Andalusian mother, a woman whose untamed and insatiable hunger for life is covered only by a thin, brittle veneer of socially acceptable behavior.

At the center of each story is the crisis of a young person approaching adulthood, for whom adolescence means rejection and disillusionment, expulsion from Paradise, and the invasion of life by death. Morante herself drew attention to this key theme in her writing: "The transition from fantasy to consciousness (from youth to maturity) is a tragic and fundamental experience for everyone. For me that experience came early and took the form of war: my encounter with maturity was premature and hit me with devastating force." Morante's novels are like the dreams she recorded in a special diary she kept in 1938 (published posthumously as *Diario*): They transport our lives, enriched by the power of the imagination, to a different reality.

Already in the diary, the image of the writer Alberto Moravia—whom Morante met in 1936 and with whom she lived until 1962—is repeatedly blocked out by that of her mother. Female generosity of spirit is contrasted with male self-centeredness. Morante responded to her damaged female identity by presenting her own archetype of femininity. Her literary works reveal it to us in all its ambivalence: a comforting protectiveness embracing children and animals, alongside a threatening, uncontrollable wildness.

ELSA MORANTE
Undated photograph

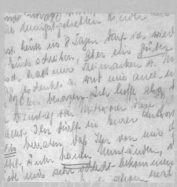

Writing as Resistance
WOMEN OF COURAGE

"Sometimes the war fills me with horror and I lose all hope of a better future. I don't even want to think about it, but it's getting so that there is nothing but politics, and as long as it goes on being so confused and so evil, it's cowardly to ignore it." These words were written by the nineteen-year-old Sophie Scholl in April 1940. But the sort of "politics" that provoked a young woman first to get involved and then to engage in resistance had little to do with the normal civic activity that the term had once signified. Politics had become something brutal and alien, something confused and evil that absolutely prevented one from carrying on with life as normal—unless one was as cowardly and apathetic as the Germans were, according to the second leaflet produced by the young members

of the White Rose group: "Why does the German nation remain so apathetic in the face of all these appalling, inhuman crimes? Hardly anyone gives them a second thought. The facts are just accepted as facts and promptly forgotten about ... Does this mean that Germans have been brutalized in their most basic human feelings, that there is nothing in them that will scream in protest at such deeds ...?"

In retrospect, the actions of Sophie Scholl, her brother Hans, and their comrades might today be considered reckless. A coward succumbs to fear and shuts his or her eyes to things or runs away, but the reckless individual fears nothing and rushes headlong into danger. Yet this is precisely what Hans and Sophie did not do. They were very well aware of the risks they were taking.

They had a firm idea of what was right, and acted in pursuit of a just cause. In short, they had courage. And if today we do not prize that particular virtue, or even understand what it is, that should give us cause for concern. What we call "having the courage of your convictions," which we do seem to value more highly, and by which we usually mean taking positive action instead of just standing on the sidelines, is of little use if courage in the true sense of the word is lacking when civil and political rights are under threat.

The decline in our appreciation of courage—which is, after all, one of the cardinal virtues, alongside wisdom, justice, and moderation—probably has to do with the fact that even the ancient world viewed it as a manly virtue. Not only feelings but also virtues are influenced by our sex, although not in a way that is fixed for all time. Gentleness has traditionally been seen as a typically womanly virtue. But what can gentleness achieve without courage when it becomes necessary to defend the rights of women, or even the rights of all human beings? Mary Wollstonecraft, for example, saw courage as the necessary precondition for achieving the "natural right" of freedom. For one can only win freedom by acting as a free person—and that is always dangerous.

IRÈNE NÉMIROVSKY
Photograph, 1933

IRÈNE NÉMIROVSKY

*I*t is rare for a publisher to be so impressed with a manuscript that he makes an instant decision to publish, but that is what happened in 1929 when the Paris publisher Bernard Grasset received the novel *David Golder*, which had been sent to him anonymously. Who was the author of this sobering story about a man in the world of high finance whose fortune collapses, burying beneath it his social influence and the affection of his family and friends? Grasset issued an advertisement asking the author to make himself known. He was most surprised when a few days later a young woman, Irène Némirovsky, who was just twenty-six years old, came forward. She had been living in France for only ten years, her family having settled there after fleeing the Russian Revolution. As a child, despite having an opulent lifestyle and being taught by governesses, Némirovsky was neglected by her parents. And so she read a great deal and began to write at the age of thirteen.

After the German occupation of France in 1940, Némirovsky and her husband, Michel Epstein, who was also Russian by birth, were forbidden to pursue their professions because they were Jews and foreigners. Although Némirovsky was very well known as a writer, she had never obtained French citizenship. In the fall of 1939, she and her husband had placed their two daughters, for safety, in a small town in Burgundy, and in 1941, they joined them there. During the previous year, Némirovsky had begun a new novel, *Suite française*, which was to be a thousand pages long and to give an uncompromising portrayal of everyday life in France under the occupation. She was able to finish the first two parts, *A Storm in June* and *Dolce*. But on July 13, 1942, she was arrested and deported to Auschwitz, where she died a few weeks later. The manuscript, packed in a suitcase together with other mementos of their mother, accompanied Némirovsky's daughters on their flight through France. Only decades later did Denise discover that the papers were not just notes but her mother's *magnum opus*. In 2004, *Suite française* was published in France and was an enormous success.

ANNE FRANK

*I*n the family's hiding-place at the back of a building in Amsterdam, a Jewish girl kept a diary from June 1942 until August 1944—from her thirteenth birthday until the day the Frank family and others living with them were discovered and Anne was taken to a concentration camp. She made the diary into a friend whom she called Kitty, and wrote her entries in the form of letters to her. "Years after the war, won't it seem ... unbelievable when we tell of how we Jews lived, talked, and ate in here?" she asks Kitty. The writer Ernst Schnabel responded with another question: "Isn't it even more unbelievable that ... they murdered this child, while we were living and talking and eating ... and six million others, and we knew, but said nothing, or we didn't know, and didn't believe what we *did* know, and now we go on living and eating and talking?"

ANNE FRANK
Photograph, *c.* 1940

SOPHIE SCHOLL

1921–1943

SOPHIE SCHOLL
Undated photograph

*S*ophie Scholl was not a writer in the usual sense of the word. She wrote love letters, kept a diary, wrote short stories—the sort of thing that young women of her generation did, giving expression to their feelings and their ideas about life. But by the time her last letter reached her boyfriend in a field hospital—he had been wounded at Stalingrad—she had already been executed. Just four days elapsed between Scholl's arrest and the execution, four long days during which she had to undergo endless interrogation. For Scholl, a member of the anti-Nazi student resistance group the White Rose, was a writer after all. She wrote and distributed leaflets that proclaimed such things as "Every word that comes out of Hitler's mouth is a lie." And "If enough people join together, then with one last mighty effort we can shake off this system."

LILLI JAHN

Above: Letter from Jahn to her children from Breitenau labor camp, October 3, 1943

LILLI JAHN
Photograph, 1918

"I will go on being brave, grit my teeth and think of you and keep going, however hard it gets." This was a mother writing in March 1944 to her five children, aged between sixteen and three. When Lilli Jahn wrote this, she was in Dresden, a stopping-point for a mass transport on its way to Auschwitz. "We hear very contradictory things about what it is like there," she tells the children; they must please not worry if they hear nothing from her for some time. The next, and last, time they heard from their mother was on June 5; two weeks later, she died in Auschwitz.

Jahn's letters tell the story of a middle-class Jewish woman, as old as the century she lived in, whose life was gradually destroyed by National Socialism. Lilli Jahn was ordinary, in the best sense of the word. She had the self-confidence common to many assimilated Jews living in Germany in the first third of the twentieth century. She was one of only fifty girls of her year group in the country to attend a *Gymnasium*, or grammar school; after that, she studied medicine and, unlike her future husband, who was also a physician, she gained a university doctorate. Her professional prospects were by no means less promising than his. Nevertheless, for him it went without saying that she, as his wife, had to give up her profession. As Lilli put it in a letter, "with a wave of his hand" he dismissed things "that have become a part of myself." An element of this self was her participation in a sophisticated, educated middle-class culture; she admired and emulated letter-writers "such as Rahel Varnhagen and Caroline Schelling."

Jahn's non-Jewish husband, having formed a relationship with a doctor colleague, who was also non-Jewish, divorced Lilli in 1942—even though he must have known that this would place her in mortal danger. The mayor of the small town reported cynically to his superior: "If the Jewish woman were deported, the Aryan woman doctor could continue to run Dr. Jahn's household ... And in that way we would be rid of the last remaining Jewish woman here."

Antek Grossa. Cöln. 1918.

In Paris and New York
REINVENTING A LIFE

"I am writing this in a tiny room in Paris, sitting on a wicker chair at a typing table in front of a window which looks out on to a garden ... That I have been living and working for more than a year in such small, bare quarters ... undoubtedly answers to some need to strip down, to close off for a while, to make a new start with as little as possible to fall back on." In the early 1970s, Susan Sontag, whose fame as a critic had already spread far beyond the shores of North America, withdrew to a little Parisian room in order to discover her own voice as a writer. This was not her first attempt at a fresh start: At the age of twenty-six, Sontag, a graduate of prestigious universities, had arrived in New York, newly divorced, holding her child by the hand, with little luggage and still less money in

her pocket, hoping to make a name for herself in the capital of pop culture.

New York and Paris—those choices were no accident. Yet Sontag was well aware that the aura of Paris as an inspiration for writers was already little more than a legend. The Paris of the "lost generation"—as Gertrude Stein, one of the first expatriates, had dubbed the group of American writers who fled there during and after the First World War—had receded into history; the Paris of the women of the Left Bank, with the lesbian salon of the American multimillionairess Natalie Barney, was just being rediscovered; the Paris of the Surrealists surrounding André Breton was almost forgotten; the most recent literary peak seemed to be the existentialist phase of the 1940s and 1950s, the Paris of Albert

Camus, Jean-Paul Sartre, Simone de Beauvoir, Boris Vian, and Juliette Gréco.

What was it that made New York and Paris so attractive to writers, women and men alike, seeking a style of life that suited them? Many were trying to escape from the narrowness of their provincial origins or from a bourgeois marriage. They were rebelling against traditional patterns of behavior, or were wanting to break with their past—and in the sophisticated milieu of New York or Paris, they found kindred spirits, as well as stages on which to experiment and try out new lifestyles. Many, among them Anaïs Nin, have described the electrically charged atmosphere that existed among the artists, for whom neither their origins nor the future counted, but only the exciting present. New York and Paris became legendary because in those cities, for both men and women, it seemed possible to do anything at all, even to reinvent one's own life and, for a short time at least, to realize the dream of being one's own creator and of living entirely in accordance with one's own wishes.

DOROTHY PARKER
Photograph, November 1941

DOROTHY PARKER

ritics called her "the wittiest woman in America." In Dorothy Parker we find a modern, more malicious form of that female wit and shrewdness that were so characteristic of Jane Austen and her heroines. Parker was a member of the Round Table, a literary circle that met in the 1920s at the Algonquin Hotel in New York, and she became famous for her acerbic wit. Her quickness at repartee earned her a reputation as a "smartcracker," but she rightly refused to be identified with the rising class of cheap humorists who were constantly tossing off jocular remarks on topical issues. For her, wit was based on knowledge and had to do with criticizing the ills of society. Parker's marriage to a stockbroker who was fonder of the bottle than of her "only lasted five minutes." She married her second husband, the actor and scriptwriter Alan Campbell—with whom she also collaborated—twice over, and they also twice separated. Depression and alcoholism led to several suicide attempts, and at the age of seventy-three, she died a lonely death in a New York hotel.

Parker began her writing career as a caption writer for *Vogue* and went on to write theater reviews for *Vanity Fair*. In 1925, she started writing for the newly founded *New Yorker* magazine, where she was put in charge of literary criticism and had her own column, "The Constant Reader," until 1933. Parker also wrote poetry—her first volume of poems, *Enough Rope* (1926), was a bestseller—as well as plays, film scripts, and above all her famous short stories. These focus on the conventional roles of the sexes and their consequences—opportunities stifled, lives destroyed. Parker wrote about nightbirds, drifters, rough sleepers, desperate lovers. Her first collection of stories, published in 1930, was entitled *Laments for the Living*.

CARSON MCCULLERS

"*D*eath is always the same, but each man dies in his own way." This is the opening sentence of Carson McCullers's final novel, *Clock Without Hands*. The pharmacist Malone, who shares his name with a character in a Samuel Beckett novel (Beckett's *Malone Dies* appeared in 1951, *Clock Without Hands* ten years later), is told by his doctor that he has only a year to live. What is the reaction of the pharmacist, who is just "an ordinary, simple man," to the knowledge of his approaching death? Time, for him, is no longer the time measured by the clock, but a period, a fixed term. This creates a distance between him and his wife and neighbors, whose response is one of denial. The isolation of the individual is McCullers's great theme; here, in her last book, it offers the opportunity to cease being ruled by the demands and expectations of other people. McCullers's earlier protagonists, usually victims of social discrimination, were rebels with a good cause but without means; their vain struggle gave such novels as *The Heart is a Lonely Hunter* (1940) a sense of hopelessness. "The greatest danger, that of losing one's own self, may pass off quietly as if it were nothing," wrote the philosopher Søren Kierkegaard, and McCullers has her Malone read that sentence and act upon it.

There had been a clock without hands in American literature once before. In a story by William Faulkner, an embittered woman who has had a stroke literally pulls the hands off her clock. McCullers suffered her first stroke in 1941, at the age of twenty-four; further strokes followed six years later, causing paralysis down one side of her body. Operations proved unsuccessful, and in the final years of her life, McCullers was bedridden. She often doubted whether she would be able to finish *Clock Without Hands*. And yet, in her very last year, McCullers was planning a study of individuals who had "triumphed over adversity." She, who had been blessed with success at a young age but had continued her work in a constant struggle with illness and loneliness, would surely have deserved a prominent place in it.

CARSON MCCULLERS
Photograph, 1959

MARGUERITE YOURCENAR

*M*arguerite Yourcenar was the first woman to be elected (in 1980) to membership of the Académie Française, although naturally not without opposition. One opponent was the anthropologist Claude Lévi-Strauss. "One does not change the rules of a tribe," he is reported to have said, using an appropriately structuralist argument. Yourcenar's gender, not her nationality, was the cause of concern among the Immortals (the academy members). The daughter of a Belgian mother and a French father, the dandy and adventurer Michel de Crayencour, Yourcenar had taken American citizenship in 1947. Ever since the beginning of the Second World War she had been living with her partner, Grace Frick, in a farmhouse on the New England coast. Exceptionally, through an intervention by the French Ministry of Justice, her French citizenship was restored, even though she never again took up permanent residence in France.

Yourcenar's justly most famous work is *Memoirs of Hadrian* (1951). Thomas Mann praised the "tantalizing authenticity of the fiction" as well as its "extremely sound basis" in historical scholarship. The project, conceived early in the author's life, was pursued through many drafts, some of which she destroyed. It was a visit that she made as a twenty-year-old to the Villa Adriana outside Rome that first suggested to her the idea of writing an account of the much-traveled emperor's life—an account that he, as a man of the second century AD, might have written himself. Added to this there was an "unforgettable" sentence from Flaubert: "Just when the gods had ceased to be, and the Christ had not yet come, there was a unique moment in history, between Cicero and Marcus Aurelius, when man stood alone." A large part of her life, Yourcenar said, "was going to be spent in trying to define, and then to portray, this man existing alone and yet closely bound with all being." Returning to the project again and again, she tried to convey the essence of a life that could lean neither on a belief in the universe of the ancient myths nor on the solace of the Christian religion. For us, with our postmythical and postreligious view of humankind, such an undertaking is eminently relevant and significant.

MARGUERITE YOURCENAR
Photograph, 1980s

ANAÏS NIN

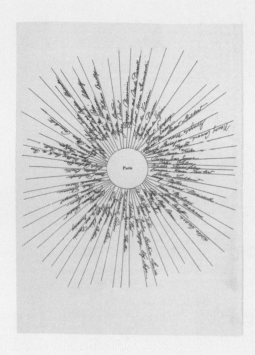

ANAÏS NIN
Undated photograph

Above: Diagram by Nin representing her friendships
and connections during her years in Paris

naïs Nin's *Diary* was written in Paris in the 1930s, but published a whole generation later and in the New World, to which Nin had returned shortly before the outbreak of the Second World War. The publication of the first volume in 1966 (covering the years 1931–34) coincided with a great shift toward a new, nonconformist lifestyle; the struggle for self-realization, the overcoming of male rationality, and sexual liberation were the burning themes of the day. And Nin's *Diary*, marketed by the publisher as a journey through the labyrinths of the self, was a mirror in which many readers who had sought a new way of life could see themselves reflected.

Both the American writer Henry Miller and his wife, June, play a crucial role in Nin's *Diary*, the author having had a passionate affair with each of them. Miller ranked the diary with the works of St. Augustine, Petronius, Abelard, Rousseau, Proust, and others, and even back in 1937, he had given the definitive indication of how it should be read—as an expression of the struggle for freedom and of a compelling search for truth.

During Nin's lifetime a decision was made to publish only those diary entries dating from 1931 onward. This was the year of Nin's meeting with Miller, the point at which the diary switched from recording her inner life to recording a life of sensual passion. Heavily edited for publication, the entries give an incomplete picture, to put it mildly, of Nin's life in Paris. The reader is led to believe that the woman who wrote them was wholly self-reliant, whereas in reality she was living with her husband, Hugh Guiler, and being supported by him, while he knew nothing of his wife's unconventional activities. Later, while living with Guiler in New York, Nin frequently went to stay in California on the pretext of needing peace and quiet for her writing. In fact, she had bigamously married a man sixteen years her junior, Rupert Pole, with whom she had set up house there—and he for his part had no idea that she was already married. Whatever our sympathies for the men concerned, this insincerity undermines the *Diary*'s claim to authenticity.

SIMONE DE BEAUVOIR

Simone de Beauvoir often argued using opposites, and would define her own position more clearly by commenting on others' designs for living. Thus she told of her mixed feelings when reading Anaïs Nin's *Diary*. She could identify with the attempt to find oneself in the past, but she disliked Nin's "narcissism": "Everything in me revolts against her conception of the woman's role." What did the author of *The Second Sex* (1949) propose as an alternative?

Nin felt that a woman's creative power lay in her closeness to nature, which men both craved and feared. De Beauvoir saw this as an attempt to create a mystique around women. "For a woman the point is not to prove herself as a woman," she writes in *All Said and Done* (1972), the fourth and final volume of her remarkable memoirs, "but to be acknowledged as a 'whole,' 'complete' human being." The fact that she succeeded in this—side by side with her fellow writer Jean-Paul Sartre, with whom she had an indissoluble bond, despite the many affairs in which they both engaged—had much to do with a way of life, based on reason, that was intended to be permanent. This was partly why she rejected Nin's plan for living, which was characterized by self-idealization and the constant breaching of norms. For de Beauvoir, life was "an undertaking with a clear goal"; to attain this, one had to look reality in the face and acknowledge that life was hard. She chose her words with care, especially when speaking of her contract with Sartre: "I have taken great pains to see that our relationship did not change, and have considered carefully what things on his part or on my part I should accept or reject, in order to avoid jeopardizing it."

De Beauvoir knew that as a writer she lacked the brilliance of someone like Virginia Woolf, but, she asserted, that was not her aspiration. Her yardstick and her theme was the awareness of her own presence in the world, and she once summed up her life as a writer in these terms: "I wanted to make others know that I existed by conveying to them, in as direct a manner as I could, the flavor of my own life: in that I have more or less succeeded."

SIMONE DE BEAUVOIR
Photograph, November 1945

MARGUERITE DURAS

$\mathcal{L}$ike Karen Blixen and Anaïs Nin, Marguerite Duras was obsessed with the idea of transforming her life into myth through the medium of art. She achieved this in 1984, when she was seventy years old, with the publication of her novel *The Lover*, which was a worldwide success. As she had done in earlier writings, Duras turned back the pages to her childhood and youth in French Indochina (present-day Vietnam), which during the period in question did not evoke memories of war and horror in the minds of Europeans but was a French colony that conjured up images of an enticing, exotic world.

All the elements of Duras's highly idiosyncratic œuvre are gathered in this book: a daughter's love–hate relationship with her mother, her fear of the brutal son of her mother's first marriage, her closeness to her younger brother and his death, the child's longings and attempts to escape. These themes are mingled with the story of the fourteen-year-old girl and her older Chinese lover. Probably the only element of biographical truth in the novel is that Duras's impoverished family did encourage her relationship with a rich man in order to get their hands on some cash. In this, more than in any of her other books, the author has set out to create a puzzle. Was it prostitution, or was it love? Is love nothing but lies and deception, or is there more to it than illusion? Is the capricious young girl really the author herself? Did the unfortunate Chinese lover really exist? *The Lover* not only raises these questions without answering them, but also sets out deliberately to make reality slide over into invention and invention into reality. Corresponding to the image of *her* ravaged face at the beginning is *his* voice at the end, saying "that it was just as before, that he still loved her, that he would never stop loving her, he would love her until death." Time, for Duras, never has ennobling or maturing powers; it is the great destroyer. Literature, on the other hand, makes time stand still so that everything becomes the present—an effect comparable to that of alcohol, on which the author had become dependent.

Duras, whose real name was Donnadieu (Duras was the name of the French village from where her father's family came), wrote both coolly and sensuously, combining Flaubert's

MARGUERITE DURAS
Photograph by Robert Doisneau
(1912–1994), 1955

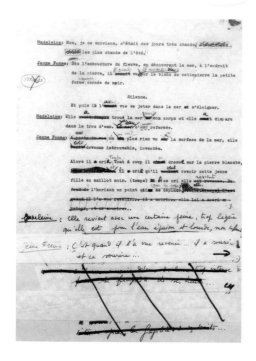

Above: Typescript of *Savannah Bay* (1982), with handwritten amendments

MARGUERITE DURAS
Undated photograph

"impassiveness," the detachment of the observer looking back, with the heat of the confessional tone and with melodramatic effects, especially when writing of the heart's passion and the passion of the flesh. She wrote, as she herself said, to transfer her own self into the book, not to obliterate it. To "massacre, waste, ruin oneself in giving birth to the book" was one side of the process; the other was that the book became an "I-object" in which any clues as to which elements in the narrative were factually true and which invented were eliminated. This deliberate ambiguity is also a result of the way in which, throughout her life, Duras rewrote and recast her memories.

Duras was exceptional among twentieth-century women writers in using film as a narrative medium on a par with the novel. She wrote movie dialogue and complete screenplays—most famously for *Hiroshima mon amour* (1959)—and directed films herself, including *India Song* (1975) and *Le Camion* (1977), with the young Gérard Depardieu. *Entire Days in the Trees* (1954) became a book, a play, and a film. Duras took some of the characteristics of each medium to develop an evocative, magical narrative style. "The aim is not to achieve something, but to break free of everything that already exists": This statement sums up an anarchic program that rejects not only the bourgeois way of life but also any way of life based on the principle of free choice. Many of Duras's heroes and heroines try to escape their isolation through unconditional love, madness, or crime; others wait—generally in vain—"for something to emerge from the world and come toward them."

Duras left Indochina for good when she was eighteen and went to France. In 1939, she married the writer Robert Antelme, who was arrested by the Gestapo in 1944 and returned to Paris in 1945 from Dachau concentration camp a dying man. Both of them based books on their memories of this time: Antelme wrote *The Human Race* (1947) and Duras *La Douleur* (1985).

FRANÇOISE SAGAN

*F*rançoise Sagan once said that the most important thing for a writer was to find the right rhythm and tone, and in *Bonjour Tristesse*, her first and most famous novel, published in 1954, she succeeded admirably. In this book, written by an eighteen-year-old, François Mauriac found "an incomparable vibrancy, a pulse, a soul, audibility without loudness." Here the earnestness of existentialism dissolves into a bittersweet mingling of moods. And moods are an expression of something that we have no power to control, the lowest layer, as it were, of the psyche; it is to this part of ourselves, largely inaccessible to thought, that art and music have always appealed.

Sagan turned to literature for both the title of her novel and her pen name: Her upper-middle-class parents had insisted that she adopt a pseudonym. Princess Boson de Sagan is a character in Marcel Proust's *Remembrance of Things Past*, while "Bonjour tristesse" is the second line of the poem "A peine défigurée" ("Barely Disfigured") by Paul Éluard (the first line is "Adieu tristesse"). *Tristesse* (sadness or sorrow) comes and goes; it is inscribed in the lines of the ceiling or in the eyes of the beloved, but it is not misery, and there is no despair in it. On the contrary, it draws attention away from terrible and monstrous aspects of human life, as Sagan's story illustrates, for the seventeen-year-old central figure, wrapped in her gentle pain, does actually drive someone to her death. Much to the author's surprise, however, it was not this but the premarital sex in the novel that provoked the scandal that helped make it a best-seller. Yet it would be unfair to suggest that this was the sole reason for the book's success. Rather, Sagan had captured a mood that no one could easily avoid in the years after the Second World War: the *tristesse* of all those who had escaped the horror and now had to live the lie that they bore none of the responsibility, but had been mere innocent bystanders.

FRANÇOISE SAGAN
Photograph taken for the cover of
Der Spiegel magazine, March 26, 1958

Love and Art are the Same the World Over

WOMEN'S VOICES IN WORLD LITERATURE

"Love's the same the world over," we read in a key passage of Doris Lessing's celebrated novel *The Golden Notebook*. This realization, acknowledged with a laugh, leads on to another, namely that a new task confronts the artist. The central character of the novel is a woman writer whose creativity is paralyzed because, as a tiny, fragile individual, she feels incapable of finding an adequate literary response to the overwhelming challenges posed by war, sickness, and the destruction of the environment. The artist as a "monstrously isolated, monstrously narcissistic, pedestalled paragon" is of no use in this situation. What is needed is a different, less strained, less self-referential notion of creativity. Lessing considers that this new kind of creativity first emerged as a mass phenomenon in the new

avant-garde and protest movements of the 1960s: "They have abolished that isolated, creative, sensitive figure—by copying him in hundreds and thousands."

Like a number of her contemporaries, Lessing was for a time a Marxist; in retrospect she saw Marxism as "the first attempt ... outside the formal religions, at a world-mind, a world ethic." But it ran a great risk of sacrificing "the driving painful individuality of ... art" on the altar of collectivism and the struggle for a better world. This was also one reason why, in the last resort, Lessing always had reservations about the women's movement. In *The Golden Notebook*, her heroine, Anna Wulf, starts to stammer as she tries to deliver a lecture urging a return to a view of art as something communal rather than

: Non, je me souviens, c'était des jours très chauds. ~~~~~~~~ les ~~~~~~ les plus chauds de l'été.

me: Dès l'embouchure du fleuve, en découvrant la mer, à l'endroit de la pierre, il ~~aurait~~ vu sur le blanc de cettepierre la petite forme cernée de noir.

Silence.

Et puis il l'~~~~~~ vue se jeter dans la mer ~~et~~ s'éloigner.

: Elle ~~~~~~~~~~ troué la mer ~~~~~son corps et elle ~~~~~~t disparu dans le trou d'eau. ~~~~~~~~ s'est refermée.

me: ~~A perte de vue~~ on ~~~~ plus rien vu ~~sur~~ la surface de la mer, elle ~~~~~~~ devenue introuvable, inventée.

individual. This is the reservation, and the stammer, of the writer who knows that there is no going back from subjectivity, which is the very seedbed of literature. It is therefore essential to arrive at a correct understanding of subjectivity and its place in the wider context.

"At last I understood," writes Lessing, "that nothing is personal, in the sense that it is uniquely one's own." One must see the individual as a "microcosm," thereby "making the personal general," she reasons, concluding that "Growing up is after all only the understanding that one's unique and incredible experience is what everyone shares." Not only love but literature, too, is intersubjective, international, and—in Lessing's view—intersexual: World literature may be written by men and increasingly by women, but it is the property of all humankind, regardless of nationality, race, or sex and, as such, it is indivisible.

DORIS LESSING

BORN 1919

*D*oris Lessing was born in what was then Persia (now Iran) and grew up in Rhodesia (present-day Zimbabwe); since 1949, she has lived in London. She published her most famous work, *The Golden Notebook*, in 1962. Women readers all over the world found in it an authentic delineation of their own experience, and recognized the main character, Anna Wulf—disappointed by men, growing less secure in her political beliefs, and suffering from writer's block—as one of their own. The novel became a feminist icon, a fact that Lessing still finds ironic. Not that she did not support the aims of the women's movement, but she had no wish to be claimed as its Messiah figure, and although *The Golden Notebook* is a novel of ideas, it is not a book with a program. It has as its frame, or skeleton, a story called "Free Women," which portrays the crisis that Anna—a woman in her thirties, the divorced mother of a daughter, and at present receiving psychotherapy—is going through. Set into this framework are long extracts from Anna's writings, which, out of fear of the chaotic state of her mind, she separates into four notebooks. The black notebook records her memories of South Africa, the red one her political activities in London; the yellow one contains ideas and sketched-out plans for books she might write, and the blue one the day-to-day events in her personal life. A passionate love affair, the subject of a fifth, the golden, notebook, is finally the means by which both Anna and her lover achieve self-healing.

Lessing's work is noticeably influenced by the psychologist Carl Jung's concept of "individuation," according to which life crises are episodes of development resulting in an expansion of consciousness. An anachronistic stage of consciousness is painfully sloughed off, and through this process, if conditions are favorable, the personality attains a new unity. This is also the schema of Lessing's fantastical and visionary books, for example *Memoirs of a Survivor* (1975), which was written at a time when the sense of impending catastrophe was perhaps at its most acute in the Western world.

DORIS LESSING
Undated photograph

PAULA FOX

BORN 1923

The legendary freewheeling lifestyle of the 1920s and 1930s has had no shortage of chroniclers, but only the American author Paula Fox has described what it was like to be a child caught up in it. In *Borrowed Finery* (2001), a memoir of her childhood and adolescence, she recalls how she led a totally disjointed life, shuttled from one place to another after being left by her parents at an orphanage only days after her birth. Her father was an alcoholic and a third-rate scriptwriter, her mother a narcissistic and capricious woman all too eager to be rid of the unwanted baby. Their circumstances were constantly changing, and every so often they would come bursting into the child's life and drag her away from a setting in which she had just begun to feel secure and to which she desperately tried to cling, knowing that it was "a lifeline that might slip out of my hands at any moment." That was the downside of her parents' free, unfettered life, in which they pursued fleeting opportunities and grand passions. We also hear about the "good" side, with its dubious glamour and swagger. Returning from a trip to Europe that had lasted several years, her parents impressed the adolescent Fox as being beautiful, "like film stars." But it soon became obvious that this was glamour on credit. Fox's father gave her a typewriter as a present, but shortly afterward took it to the pawnshop. She never saw it again.

All the same, Fox did become a writer, although her first novel was not published until she was forty-three and at last living a more settled life. Telling stories became her method of discovering how little substance there is in the established attitudes and so-called truths that have been passed down the generations. As well as six novels, Fox has written many books for children and teenagers, which for some time enjoyed far greater success than her adult books. Her novels became popular only in the late 1990s, when a new generation of American writers began to take her tragic realism as their model.

TONI MORRISON
Photograph, November 1993

TONI MORRISON

*E*ver since she began writing, Toni Morrison, who in 1993 became the first African American woman to be awarded the Nobel Prize for Literature, has wanted her books to be accessible to everyone—to the reader without preconceptions who simply wants to fall under the spell of a book's atmosphere, plot, and language, as well as to the more intellectual reader who is aware of literary traditions. There had been no such tradition for African Americans: Morrison has created one. However, she has never addressed herself specifically to an African American readership. Her literary intelligence, she says, is without gender, nationality, or race. Imagination is free of all such labels.

As the key to her writing, Morrison points to the improvisations of black jazz musicians, making their wild, angry, but also highly complex and seductive music without adjusting it to conform to the white idiom. Improvisation has nothing to do with an absence of rules. According to the black pianist Cecil Taylor, it represents a supreme degree of self-awareness, but awareness of the self in relation to others. Morrison models her writing on this approach, creating a multivoiced, pulsating, and rhythmic prose that is as sophisticated, subtle, bold, and controlled as black music. Her novel *Jazz* (1992) is an incomparable tribute to this source of her art.

Morrison's four most recent novels form a cycle on the theme of love. At the heart of *Beloved* (1987), which depicts the era of slavery and its legacy from the point of view of its victims, is a mother's love. *Jazz*, set in the black Harlem of the 1920s, is the story of a love triangle, a depiction of passion with all its hidden depths and violence. *Paradise* (1997), with a plot reaching into the 1970s, is a novel about the love of God, posing the question of why utopian ideals always involve exclusion. And finally, *Love* (2003) is set in the 1990s, and celebrates a kind of love that is superior to other kinds, an all-embracing *caritas* that "envieth not, vaunteth not itself, is not puffed up, and never faileth."

ASSIA DJEBAR

At the age of twenty, Fatma-Zohra Imalayen from Algeria signed her first contract with a Parisian publisher. From then on, she used the pseudonym Assia Djebar because her book contained erotic elements, and she did not want to upset her Muslim parents.

"Writing about yourself puts you in mortal danger," Djebar once said in an interview. As an Algerian woman who had passed through the French education system, she felt herself to be in a vulnerable position in any case. Writing her first novels represented a disengagement both from her surroundings and from herself. This disengagement had begun while she was still a schoolgirl. Asked why his daughters did not wear the veil, her father is said to have replied, "Because they read"—in other words, because they were studying. But Djebar finally came to realize that in trying to distance herself as far as possible from her own self, she was merely following the rules laid down by her mother and other relatives: "First, never speak about yourself, and secondly, if that proves absolutely impossible, then at least speak 'anonymously.'" "Speaking anonymously means never using the first person."

For ten years, Djebar published nothing, but instead began to make films. *The Nouba of the Women of Mount Chenoua* (1979) was a film about the peasant women of the Algerian hinterland that she produced and directed herself, as well as writing the script. In 1980, she resigned from her post at Algiers University and left Algeria for good, "because I, a woman, wanted to write." Her cycle of stories *Women of Algiers in Their Apartment*, published in the same year, was her first response to the policy of Arabization in Algeria, and was intended as a preliminary to a film project. But the way of seeing that Djebar had developed as a filmmaker gave her, as a writer, too, a sense of control and a variable viewpoint that can switch between the two cultures in which she grew up. "I write in order to travel through myself," she says, quoting the author and painter Henri Michaux, but adds, "looking for yesterday's enemy, whose language I have stolen." In 2005, Djebar was made a member of the Académie Française.

ASSIA DJEBAR
Undated photograph

ISABEL ALLENDE
Photograph, October 1996

ISABEL ALLENDE

*T*he Chilean writer Isabel Allende is far more of an international celebrity than her Algerian counterpart Assia Djebar. She owes her prominence partly to her name— President Salvador Allende, assassinated in the military coup of 1973, was a cousin of her father's—and partly to the tried-and-tested recipe of magic realism, which she dilutes for her own purposes. Her work, like that of Djebar, has at its core the conflict of cultures and the liberating power of writing, with its capacity to blend memory and detachment.

"You've got a lot to do, so stop feeling sorry for yourself, drink some water, and start writing," is the advice given to Alba, a young woman who has been tortured, in Allende's novel *The House of the Spirits* (1982). Encouraged by the success of this first novel, Allende heeded this advice herself: To date, she has written nine novels and three books for young people, and her rate of output is visibly increasing. *Eva Luna* (1987), her third novel, was the story of the rise of a young woman from poverty to prominence as a writer of television soap operas. There may have been an element of self-irony in this, since Allende herself has written for television, although her own background was that of a diplomat's family. What is also ironic is her inversion of the story of the biblical Fall, which serves as a subtext to the history of the Latin American continent: Eva is the daughter of a European woman who found herself in the jungle and an Indian who had been bitten by a snake.

By the time Allende wrote *The Infinite Plan* (1991), she was living in California with her second husband, an American. The novel contrasts Anglo-Saxon culture with the subculture of the Indians. In *Paula* (1994), a personal memoir, the author recounts her own life story to her daughter, who is lying in a coma, in the hope of postponing and perhaps even outwitting death, like Scheherazade. But Paula is never going to regain consciousness, and the narrator finally has to accept that the chain of transmission from one generation to the next has been broken.

ZERUYA SHALEV

BORN 1959

*T*he title of Paula Fox's novel *Desperate Characters* (1970; for the entry on Fox, see pages 138–39) suggests people driven to despair, but also people who will stop at nothing. A chamber piece about a crumbling marriage, the book subsequently became a model for many other authors. Fox herself once said that her novels suited the harsher view of things taken by a younger generation. When, in *Desperate Characters*, it takes only a bite from a cat to expose the shaky foundations of an apparently well-ordered existence, this is because traditional roles and models are no longer appropriate to the times, while a new set of values is still nowhere in sight.

The Israeli author Zeruya Shalev may be counted among that younger generation of writers with no illusions. Her three latest novels—*Love Life* (1997), *Husband and Wife* (2000), and *Late Family* (2005)—form a trilogy about the damaging effect that the force of sexual desire has on family life, and about destruction and new beginnings. Shalev's books are extraordinary linguistic events. Hypnotizing the reader, they simultaneously disturb and fascinate. Their female protagonists are women on the verge of a nervous breakdown who possess a bewitching sensuality. Biblical motifs, frequently introduced through the female characters, give the novels added resonance. Love means exodus, the destruction of the Temple, the Diaspora. Only in Thomas Mann's tetralogy *Joseph and His Brothers* (1933–43) has there ever before been such a complete fusion of Jewish myth and psychology as in Shalev. And yet the relationship is a different one. In Mann, the formula had been: myth plus psychology equals humanity. His characters were conscious of walking in ancient footsteps. They were at once very old and very young. Shalev adopts the opposite approach. Her starting point is the way that all our intimate relationships are now seen in psychological terms. As a catalyst, she adds the great Jewish narratives of the Old Testament. Psychology divided by myth also equals humanity, but a humanity that is terrified by its own archaic quality. We are still in flight—from our persecutors, from God, from death, from ourselves. Although we may remain youthful all our lives, we are also very old.

Zeruya Shalev
Photograph, September 2005

ARUNDHATI ROY
Photograph, September 1997

ARUNDHATI ROY

BORN 1961

*W*hat is most striking about Arundhati Roy is her energetic personality and the impossibility of impressing her. Ever since she was a little girl, says this Anglo-Indian author and activist, she knew that she wanted to be a writer. But she never supposed that it would be possible; her background seemed to rule it out. However, she always threw herself into everything she did with total commitment. At a certain point she started writing for films, and this was the start of her career as an author. "No matter what I ... do, I become absorbed in it," Roy has explained. "And that was what happened when I started writing *The God of Small Things* [1997]. ... I never spent time ... resenting my present state. No, my secret was to live my life refusing to be a victim."

People in Western societies—whether women, burned-out executives, the unemployed, or writers—increasingly define themselves as the victims of social problems. Social psychologists speak of a growing culture of victimhood. Roy, by contrast, demonstrates that true freedom lies in abandoning the role of victim. The most important thing is the decision to choose a life of freedom and action; the question of what form that action should take is secondary. On this basis, writing and political activity are of equal worth because they arise from the same latent energy in one's life—what the philospher Hannah Arendt, that great advocate of a life of action, called the "impetus of the start that birth represents." This impetus, this driving force, is what the woman in Roy's novel is trying to rediscover when she travels to India to see her former husband, at the same time traveling back to her own past. There she encounters not only the constraints of convention but also the anarchy of the modest miracles of everyday life, which are controled not by the God of History, who decrees the overall course of things, but by the God of Small Things—"the God of Goose Bumps and Sudden Smiles." He is above all the God of Loss, but also the god who offers a pact between one's own personal dream and the world of reality.

PICTURE CREDITS

Jacket, front: picture-alliance/KPA/HIP/ Ann Ronan Picture Library
Jacket, back (left to right): Associated Press; picture-alliance/dpa; Archives Charmet/Bridgeman Art Library

Endpapers: akg-images/Walter Limot

pp. 1, 39 Gisèle Freund/Agence Nina Beskow

p. 4 Hatfield House, Hertfordshire

p. 5 British Library

p. 8 Lisa Yuskavage

pp. 10, 62 picture-alliance/dpa

pp. 13, 97 ullstein–Granger Collection

pp. 15, 75 ullstein–Granger Collection

p. 18 Bridgeman Art Library

pp. 21, 61 picture-alliance/dpa

p. 23 picture-alliance/KPA/HIP/ British Library

pp. 24, 68 Bridgeman Art Library

p. 26 Lauros/Giraudon/Bridgeman Art Library

pp. 29, 59 akg-images

p. 30 Bridgeman Art Library

pp. 33, 127 ullstein–Roger Viollet

pp. 36, 105 Associated Press

p. 43 picture-alliance/akg-images

p. 44 picture-alliance/akg-images/ British Library

p. 46 akg-images

p. 47 Archives Charmet/Bridgeman Art Library

p. 50 Bridgeman Art Library

p. 53 picture-alliance/akg-images

p. 54 bpk/SBB

p. 57 akg-images

p. 58 picture-alliance/akg-images

p. 60 British Library

p. 64 British Library

p. 65 Paul Barker

p. 66 picture-alliance/dpa

p. 72 picture-alliance/dpa

p. 73 Johanna-Spyri-Archiv, Zurich

p. 76 picture-alliance/akg-images/IMS

p. 77 Interfoto-Archiv

p. 79 akg-images/IMS

p. 82 Archives Charmet/Bridgeman Art Library

p. 85 Archives Charmet/Bridgeman Art Library | VG Bild-Kunst, Bonn 2006

p. 86 State Library of New South Wales, Sydney, Australia

p. 89 picture-alliance/KPA/HIP/Ann Ronan Picture Library

p. 90 akg-images

p. 91 From Detlef Brennecke, *Tania Blixen*, Reinbek, Rowohlt, 1996

p. 92 akg-images

p. 93 From Else Lasker-Schüler, *Hebräische Balladen* (*Hebrew Ballads*), edited by Norbert Oellers, Marbacher Schriften, Marbach am Neckar, Deutsches Literaturarchiv, 1986

p. 95 picture-alliance/akg-images

p. 99 ullstein–Popper Ltd

p. 100 picture-alliance/akg-images

p. 102 picture-alliance/dpa

p. 107 Effigie/Bilderberg

p. 110 ullstein–Roger Viollet

p. 112 picture-alliance/akg-images

p. 113 akg-images

pp. 114, 115 Dr. Martin Doerry, Hamburg; from Martin Doerry, *Mein verwundetes Herz: Das Leben der Lilli Jahn 1900–1944*, Munich, DVA, 2002

p. 118 Associated Press

p. 120 picture-alliance/akg-images

p. 123 ullstein–Camera Press Ltd

p. 124 Bilderberg/Effigie

p. 125 Anaïs Nin Trust

p. 128 Atelier Robert Doisneau

p. 130 Institut Mémoires de l'Édition Contemporaine (IMEC), Paris

p. 131 Bilderberg/Effigie

p. 133 akg-images

p. 137 ullstein–Camera Press Ltd

p. 139 Associated Press

p. 140 picture-alliance/dpa

p. 143 picture-alliance/dpa

p. 144 ullstein–Piel

p. 147 akg-images/Doris Poklekowski

p. 148 picture-alliance/dpa

pp. 150–51 Roger Viollet, Paris/ Bridgeman Art Library